ADULT LEARNING

ADULT LEARNING

By

Dr. E.Bhuvaneswara Choudary

Dept. of Adult & Continuing Education

S.V. University, Tirupati

(Andhra Pradesh)

(India)

DISCOVERY PUBLISHING HOUSE PVT. LTD.

NEW DELHI-110 002

Published by:
Tilak Wasan
DISCOVERY PUBLISHING HOUSE PVT. LTD.
4383/4B, Ansari Road, Darya Ganj
New Delhi-110 002 (India)
Phone : +91-11-23279245, 43596064-65
Fax : +91-11-23253475
E-mail : parul.wasan@gmail.com
discoverypublishinghouse@gmail.com
web : www.discoverypublishinggroup.com

***First Edition:* 2012**

ISBN: 978-93-5056-065-5

Adult Learning

Printed at:
Shree Balaji Art Press
Delhi

Preface

The socio-economic development of any country depends upon its educated citizens. India cannot achieve economic development, social transformation and effective social security until and unless the citizens are educated to the extent that enables them to participate in the country's developmental programmes, willingly, intelligently and effectively. Illiteracy as a mass phenomenon blocks economic and social progress, affects health and community hygiene, population control, national integration and security. Illiterate people tend to resist change and cling to traditionalistic forms of life. New ideas and new practices cannot be effectively communicated to those who are untrained to receive them and make use of them. Therefore, there is a need to reshape and change the attitude of masses through education and training. Adult Education emphasizes upon three main components namely, literacy, functionality and awareness. Literacy which is supposed to be a stepping stone for education includes the three rudimentary skills of reading, writing and numeracy and is considered as a minimum need for every human being to have a better life in the society. Functional literacy implies self-reliance in literacy and numeracy, becoming aware of the causes for their deprivation and moving towards amelioration of their conditions through organization and participation in the process of development, acquiring skills to improve the economic status and general well-being, imbibing the values of national integration, conservation of the environment, women's equality, observance of small family norms, etc. Functionality more or less is concerned with making the individual to function well individually, socially, culturally and economically. Adult education in India does not end with providing literacy, functionality and awareness. It extends further leading to life long education and continuing education. The scope of adult education extends to all sections of the community and it is a pre-condition to accelerate the pace and magnitude of development.

The Government of India and non-government organisations are making a lot of efforts to eradicate illiteracy in our country. The effective implementation of total literacy campaigns has contributed towards the substantial increase of neo-literates and semi-literates. But due to lack of immediate post-literacy activities at the grassroot level and due to lack of people's participation in the continuing education centres the neo-literates and semi-literates are again relapsing into illiteracy. The non-enrolment and dropout at primary level and at adult education centres, poor socio-economic conditions are other reasons is leading to the problem of illiteracy in the country. How to check the problem? What types of efforts are basically required to promote adult education in the country and at the global level. Studies that deal with the basic aspects of learning or achievement in relation to different personal, social, economic and programme related factors would be of immense help to the programme planners and executives to design effective strategies. The present study which is related to the on-going programme of adult education would be of greater help to the district administrations and National Literacy Mission to chalk out effective strategies for promoting the literacy, post-literacy and continuing education programmes.

The book is divided into six chapters The first chapter deals with Introduction. In the second chapter, the Review Related Literature is presented. Chapter three deals with Statement of the Problem, Objectives and Hypotheses whereas chapter four concentrates on Methodology of Investigation. In chapter Five, Analysis of Results is presented. Chapter Six deals with Summary and conclusions, Suggestions for Further Research and Implications of the study.

Dr. E. Bhuvaneswara Choudary

Dept. of Adult & Continuing Education

S.V. University, Tirupati.

Acknowledgement

I express my heartfelt gratitude to Prof. T. Kumaraswamy, M.A., M.Com, M.Ed., Ph.D., Department of Adult and Continuing Education, Sri Venkateswara University, Tirupati for his valuable guidance, enlightening discussion and critical comments during different phases of the present investigation.

I am grateful to Prof. M.C. Reddeppa Reddy, M.A., M.Ed., Ph.D., Director and Principal S.V.U. College of Education and Extension Studies, Tirupati, for his interest, timely suggestions and constant encouragement throughout this investigation.

I am thankful to Prof. P. Adinarayana Reddy, Dr. K. Sudha Rani, Dr. B. Syam Mohan David Raju, Dr. R.B. Sathyavathi, Department of Adult and Continuing Education, Sri Venkateswara University, Tirupati, for their help and constructive criticism in completing the work.

I am specially thankful to Prof. Samiullah, Department of Psychology, S.V.University, Tirupati and Prof. G. Babu Rao, Department of Psychology, S.V. University, Tirupati, for their kind suggestions.

I am thankful to Sri N. Krishnaiah, Statistician, for his kind help in computer analysis.

I express my heartful thanks to the Deputy Director of Adult Education, Project Officers, Supervisors and Mandal Literacy Organisers and Preraks of Chittoor district, for their kind co-operation.

I am grateful to the neo-literates who have served as subjects of the study for their patience and immense co-operation in collection of data.

Finally, I am indebted to my parents and sisters, Sri E. Narasimhulu Naidu, Smt. E. Janakiamma, and my Sister P. Komala, Brother-in-law P. Subodh, for their constant encouragement and support with regard to present study.

E. Bhuvaneswara Chowdary

Contents

Preface

Acknowledgement

1. Introduction **1**

Education and National Development – An Overview of Adult Education Programmes After Independence – Social Education Programme – Gram Shikshan Mohim – Farmers Functional Literacy Programme – Education Commission – Non-formal Education – Polyvalent Adult Education Centres – Adult Education for Women – Nation Adult Education Programme – Adult Education Through Universities and Colleges – Rural Functional Literacy Project – State Adult Education Programme – Adult Education Through Voluntary Agencies – Mass Programme for Functional Literacy – National Literacy Mission – Total Literacy Campaigns – Post-literacy and Continuing Education – Objectives – Functions of Continuing Education Centres – Jana Shikshan Sansthan – Profile of Chittoor District – Boundaries and Topography – Climate – Rainfall – Rivers – Soils – Minerals – Irrigation – Literacy Activities in Chittoor District – Strengths of the Campaign – The Present Study – An Overview of Succeeding Chapters.

2. Review of Related Literature **28**

Studies on Personal, Social and Economic Factors (Gender, Age, Caste, Occupation, Marital Status,

Income) – Studies on Psychological Factors – Studies on Attitude.

3. **Statement of The Problem** 68

Dependent Variables – Independent Variables – Neo-literate – Prerak – Performance/Achievement – Monitor – Functional Literacy – Adult Learners – Equivalency Programmes – Income Generating Programmes – Quality of Life Improvement Programmes – Individual Interest Promotion Programmes – Continuing Education – Post-literacy – Attitude Towards Adult Education.

4. **Methodology** 80

Measure of Achievement – I. Reading Test – II. Writing Test – III. Numeracy Test – Validity and Reliability – Measure of Personality – Measure of Attitude – Rating Procedure for the Statements – Procedure of Standardization – Scoring of the Statement – Selection of the Statements – Reliability of the Measure – Validity of the Scale – Content Validity – Item Validity – Intrinsic Validity – Selection of the Sample – Collection of Data – Analysis of Data.

5. **Results and Discussion** 96

Distribution of Writing Achievement Scores – Distribution of Numeracy Achievement Scores – Distribution of Total Achievement Scores – Gender vs. Achievement – Age vs. Achievement – Influence of Caste on Achievement – Marital Status vs. Achievement – Occupations vs. Achievement – Income vs. Achievement – Factor A vs. Achievement – Factor B vs. Achievement – Factor C vs. Achievement – Factor E vs. Achievement – Factor F vs. Achievement – Factor G vs. Achievement – Factor L vs. Achievement –

Factor M vs. Achievement—Factor N vs. Achievement—Factor Q1 vs. Achievement—Factor Q2 vs. Achievement—Factor Q3 vs. Achievement—Factor Q4 vs. Achievement—Correlation with Achievement in Reading—Correlation with Achievement in Writing—Correlation with Achievement in Numeracy—Correlation with Total Achievement—Factors Predicting Achievement of Neo-literates in Reading—Factors Predicting Achievement of Neo-literates in Writing—Factors Predicting Achievement of Neo-literates in Numeracy—Factors Predicting Total Achievement of Neo-literates.

6. Summary and Conclusions **182**

Introduction—Statement of the Problem—Need for the Study—Objectives of the Study—Hypotheses—Variables Studied—Dependent Variables—Independent Variables—Tools Developed—Selection of the Sample—Collection of Data—Analysis of Data—Findings of the Study—Implications of the Study—Suggestions for Further Research.

Bibliography **207**

Index **221**

1 Introduction

Education and National Development

The vital relationship between education and national development needs hardly to be over-emphasized. Education has all along been a powerful instrument of social, economic, political and cultural change and it thereby gave strong impetus to national development. In the ultimate process of development, the role of education is to impart knowledge, understanding, attitudes and skills to human resources and in turn make these resources qualified to utilize the physical resources fully and effectively. Probably this is why that the contribution of education to national development is being increasingly realized today more than ever before and development is now conceived primarily as a process of education. India cannot achieve economic development, social transformation and effective social security until and unless the citizens are educated to the extent that enables them to participate in the country's developmental programmes, willingly, intelligently and effectively. Illiteracy as a mass phenomenon blocks economic and social progress, affects health and community hygiene, population control, national integration and security. Illiterate people tend to resist change and cling to traditionalistic forms of life. New ideas and new practices cannot be effectively communicated to those who are untrained to receive them and make use of them.

Education today is indispensable, and is obviously a challenging task. It has become a matter of growing national debate and concern. The need for education continues to grow is evident from the increasing investment in educational programmes and corresponding demand for it. Every country develops its system of education to meet the challenges of times. Thus the developing educational system must build upon the gains of the past and the present for a better future and indeed, of mankind. The very aim of education is to develop an integrated personality, suitably stuffed and equipped from all dimensions, viz., physical, mental, moral, emotional and vocational. Education does not mean imparting verbal knowledge. The knowledge that is gathered should be capable of being used for all life situations, service to society and helping to improve the deplorable conditions of

Table 1.1 : Literacy Rate in India from 1901-2001 (Percentage)

Year	Total	Men	Women	
1901	5.35	9.83	0.60	(5 years & above)
1911	5.92	10.56	1.05	(5 years & above)
1921	7.16	12.21	1.18	(5 years & above)
1931	9.50	15.59	2.93	(5 years & above)
1941	16.10	24.90	7.30	(5 years & above)
1951	16.67	24.95	7.93	(5 years & above)
1961	24.02	34.44	12.95	(5 years & above)
1971	29.45	39.45	18.69	(5 years & above)
1981	36.23	46.89	24.52	(5 years & above)
1991	52.11	63.86	39.42	(7 years & above)
2001	65.38	75.85	54.16	(7 years & above)

one's own country. Therefore, there is a need to reshape and change the attitude of masses through education and training. Today, India is confronted with a massive number of 450 million illiterates in all age groups. Of this, about 110 million are in the 15-35 age group.

A glance at the table reveals that the growth of literacy rate has been slow upto 1951 and it has been rising at a faster level later on. Due to effective implementation of several literacy drives after independence considering the strengths and weaknesses of the programmes and by introducing better strategies the results are satisfying. However, there is a lot to be done in this direction. The literacy rate as per 2001 census is 65.38 per cent. The growth of literacy among men is better in relation to that of women and by 2001, the rate of literacy among men is 75.85 per cent and among women it stands at 54.16 per cent at national level. India accounts for 29.6 per cent of world illiterates, the biggest of its nature followed by China with 23.6 per cent. It is heartening to note that we are not able to raise literacy rate atleast by two per cent per year. Still there are imbalances in literacy rates of the country. Kerala is at the first place with 90.92 per cent while Bihar is at the last place with 47.53 per cent of literacy as per 2001 census. Regional disparities, linguistic variations, social and economic aspects-all these are accounting for variations in the growth rare of literacy in our country.

An Overview of Adult Education Programmes After Independence

Social Education Programme

In India, the government has given special attention to adult education after independence. Several programmes were formulated to combat illiteracy. Social Education Programme was taken up during 1949-50. The objectives of the programme are as follows:

- (*a*) To instill a consciousness of the rights and duties of citizenship and foster a spirit of service to the community;

(*b*) To develop a love of democracy and impart an understanding of the way in which democracy functions;

(*c*) To disseminate knowledge of the outstanding problems and difficulties facing the country and the world today;

(*d*) To develop pride in our cultural heritage through the knowledge of our history, geography and culture;

(*e*) To teach the simple laws of personal and community health and develop habits of hygiene and cleanliness;

(*f*) To foster the growth of the co-operative spirit as a way of life;

(*g*) To provide training in crafts both as a hobby and as a means to economic betterment;

(*h*) To provide cultural and recreational facilities by way of folk dances, drama, music, poetry, recitation and other ways of spontaneous self-expression;

(*i*) To provide through these various activities as well as through reading and discussion groups, an understanding of the basic moral values;

(*j*) To acquire reasonable mastery over the tools of learning, reading, writing, simple arithmetic and to create an interest in knowledge;

(*k*) To provide facilities for continuation of education through libraries, discussion groups, clubs and institutions like peoples colleges.

The content of social education is 5-fold:

1. Health and Hygiene
2. Family and Community Living
3. Vocations
4. Literacy and Cultural Activities
5. Recreational Activities

The five-fold is amplified as follows:

1. ***Health and Hygiene :*** Nutritious food and drinking water, care of body and its parts, clothing, personal cleanliness and sanitation, importance of sun, air and water, common diseases and their treatment;

2. ***Family and Community Living :*** Relationship of individual members in the family, care and welfare of children, management of the home, home economics, family in the social context, marriage etc.;

3. ***Vocations :*** (*i*) Agriculture : soil, seeds, sowing and planting, rotation of crops, seasons-manures-protection of crops, co-operatives; (*ii*) cottage industries-spinning and weaving, knitting, net making, basket making, carpentry, leather work, cane work, soap making, fruit preservation, principles of co-operation, credit and banking, buying and selling-farm products etc.;

4. ***Literacy and Cultural Activities :*** (*i*) Very simple reading, letter writing, filling in of money order forms, simple every day arithmetic; (*ii*) Elementary Knowledge of village, district, province, country and of the world, stories of great persons; (*iii*) Self-Government, duties of citizens, meaning and importance of vote, Panchayat system, local and district Boards, Municipalities, Home Legislatures; (*iv*) Laws, Social conventions and orderliness, courtesy, co-operation and tolerance; (*v*) Value of libraries;

5. ***Recreational Activities:*** Indoor and outdoor games, sports, folk dances, community singing, plays, film shows, etc.

It may be noted that due to lack of proper planning and implementation the programme could not become a success. The participation of learners was poor and the emphasis was only on imparting of literacy. The instruction was based on formal methods and supervision and monitoring were not properly planned.

Gram Shikshan Mohim

Movement for literacy in the rural areas began in 1959 in Satara district of Maharashtra and was later extended to other parts of the state. The programme aimed at imparting basic literacy skills with in a period of four months. By 1963, it spread to all the districts of the state. The programme, however, suffered from lack of systematic follow-up and consequently, relapse into illiteracy was massive. The strengths and weaknesses of the programmes were taken as the basis in designing the further programmes.

Farmers Functional Literacy Programme

Farmers' Functional Literacy Programme (FFLP) was taken up during 1966-67 with the objective of extending education and training facilities to farmers with a view to raise agricultural production. It was felt that farmers training would become meaningful, if it is treated as an essential input of programmes (along with knowledge of fertilizers, pesticides, irrigation, high yielding varieties of seeds, multiple cropping, intensive cash crops and intensive cattle development programmes. In order to make FFLP effective, the following strategy was formulated:

- Farmers education and training programmes should be co-ordinated so as to achieve quick production. All government and non-government agencies should organize their programmes according to production requirements and cropping;
- The education and training should result in the acquisition of skills for the adoption of new practices and use of inputs. At some point, there should be connection between the supply of inputs and the

imparting of training. Demonstration in the use of these skills should be an essential element of training;

- There should be two-way communication between the participating farmers and experts. This means that framers should be able to address their enquiries to experts of a level higher than the average level extension worker and get replies in writing. The radio programmes should be drawn according to the progress of the crop season and the education and training should be provided at the demonstration camps. Every aspect of the extension and education programmes should revolve around the agricultural production programmes.

The programme was successful due to participation of target group (farmers), usage of need based primers and administration of the programme. However, lack of effective post –literacy and continuing education activities and their monitoring were the main problems of the programme.

Education Commission

Constitution of Education Commission (1964-66) was a significant event in the history of education in India. Among several measures, it recommended that high priority be accorded to ending illiteracy. It urged that adult education be promoted both through 'selective' as well as through 'mass approach' and stressed the active involvement of teachers and students and the wider use of the media for the literacy programme.

The Education Commission also stated that in the world of science and technology, the main objective should be to relate it to life, needs and aspirations of the people so as to make it an instrument of socio-economic and political change. The suggestions offered were quite worthy for implementing the future programmes.

Non-formal Education

In the beginning of the Fifth plan, a programme of non-formal education for people falling in 9-14 and 15-25 years age group was launched. Although the scope, content and objectives of the non-formal project were clearly spelt out, its understanding in the field was very limited and the programmes actually organized were indistinguishable from the conventional literacy programmes.

Polyvalent Adult Education Centres

Workers social education institutes and polyvalent adult education centres were reviewed by a group in 1977, which recommended adoption of polyvalent adult education centres in the adult education programme for workers in urban areas. In pursuance of the decision, Shramik Vidyapeeths were set up in the states. The programmes were mainly limited to urban areas and could be reach majority of the neo-literate groups.

Adult Education for Women

The Government of India has launched a number of adult literacy programmes, which also cater to literacy of adult women. However, a scheme of functional literacy for women (1975) has been brought about as a high priority programme of the Department of Social Welfare. The scheme is being implemented by the Integrated Child Development Services (ICDS) project. It focuses its attention on adult women in the age group of 15 to 45 years. It (*a*) helps women to acquire skills through functional literacy classes; (*b*) imparts information on modern methods of health and hygiene and the importance of nutritious food and balanced diet; and (*c*) provides need-based training in home management and child care.

Nation Adult Education Programme

National Adult Education Programme (NAEP) was inaugurated on 2nd October, 1978 with literacy as an indispensable component, for approximately 100 million illiterate persons in the age group 15-35 with a view to providing them skills for self-directed learning leading to self-reliant and active role in their own development and in the development of their environment. Preparatory action aimed at the following areas:

- Creation of an environment favourable to the launching of NAEP;
- Preparation of case studies of some significant past experience, particularly those where the failures or successes have a bearing on the planning and implementation of NAEP;
- Detailed planning of the various segments of the programme by appointment of experts groups. This would include preparation of detailed plans for each state and union territory;
- Establishment of necessary structures for administration and co-ordination and necessary modification of procedure and patterns;
- Identification of various agencies, official and non-official, to be involved in the programme and taking necessary measures to facilitate the needed level of their involvement like Government Agencies, Universities, State Resource Centres, Voluntary Organizations etc.;
- Development of capability in all states for preparation of diversified and need based teaching / learning materials for the programme.;
- Development of training methodologies, preparation of training manuals as well as actual training of personnel at various levels to launch the programme;

- Creation of a satisfactory system of evaluation and monitoring, post-literacy as well as the required applied research base.

In addition to organizing a massive programme for adult illiterates, it was felt necessary to provide special programmes for special groups based on their special needs. For example, programmes are needed for: (*a*) urban workers to improve their skills, to prepare them for securing their rightful claims and for participation in management; (*b*) government functionaries such as office clerks, field extension workers to upgrade their competence; (*c*) employees of commercial establishments to improve their performance; and (*d*) housewives to inculcate a better understanding of family life problems and women's status in society.

Adult Education Through Universities and Colleges

Adult Education and extension through universities and colleges was taken up under Point No. 16 of the New 20 Point Programme in 1982-83. The major aspects include the following:

- Teaching, research and extension are the three basic objectives of university education and equal importance should be given to them. Extension activity should be an important dimension of higher education;
- A single mechanism needs to be created in the university system whereby all activities like adult literacy, NSS, NCC, continuing and extension programmes etc., are organized under one umbrella;
- Institutions of higher education must participate in programmes of adult literacy and contribute to the educational and other development needs of the under privileged sections of the society;
- Point No. 16 of the New 20 Point Programme also relates to the spread of universal elementary

education. The students could motivate children who are not going to schools. The university / college students from the NSS could be helpful in locating the non-school going children and getting them admitted in other primary schools or non-formal education centres. They could also organize remedial coaching classes for the needy and academically under privileged children of the society. This could be another dimension to the participation of students in the implementation of Point No. 16 of the New 20 Point Programme of the Government of India.

Rural Functional Literacy Project

This was a major centrally sponsored scheme started in 1978 in rural areas as part of National Adult Education Programme. The erstwhile 144 farmers functional literacy projects and 60 non-formal education projects were merged into it. Furthermore, new projects were added bringing the total number of projects throughout the country in 1987 to 513, each having upto a maximum number of 300 adult education centres and each centre having 25-30 learners.

State Adult Education Programme

The states also similarly took up centre based projects under the state plan funds on the lines of RFLPs. SAEP and RLFP were part of the major National Adult Education Programme.

Adult Education Through Voluntary Agencies

In order to ensure greater participation of voluntary agencies, the central scheme of assistance to voluntary agencies was revived in April, 1982. Under this scheme, registered societies were sanctioned the centre-based projects for functional literacy and post literacy, and were allowed to run projects in a compact area. The programmes became successful in a few areas but documentation remained as improper and follow up activities could not be organized effectively.

Mass Programme for Functional Literacy

Mass Programme for Functional Literacy started in 1986 aimed at involving high school and college students in imparting literacy to their illiterate relatives, parents and people residing in nearby areas during summer vacation. Mass Programme for Functional Literacy was started with the objectives of making literacy as a people's mission, harnessing all agencies for the mission and posing mass literacy programme as a challenge for the youth. Achievement of these objectives involved:

- Stressing functional literacy in National Service Scheme (NSS);
- Increasing coverage of student volunteers;
- Emphasizing study and service viz., specific project taken up by the students as part of work experience for social / national service which should be reflected in their final result; and
- Provisions for institutional incentives for eradication of illiteracy.

There was no adequate preparation for the programme. It ended upto motivating the students and the follow up activity was not there. Though there were significant contributions in some pockets yet they did not receive proper attention. Monitoring and evaluation and maintenance of records also did not receive proper attention. The experiences of National Adult Education Programme and others revealed the following limitations:

- The programmes were considered only as government programmes;
- The participation of the people and beneficiaries remained as a weak link;
- The development departments of the government did not lend active support for the programmes;

- The training programmes were organized haphazardly and remained weak;
- Finances were not released in time and even the budget provided was not used upto mark;
- The learners lacked motivation and participation;
- The monitoring, evaluation, supervision aspects remained weak;
- There was no co-ordination among the various agencies working for the cause of adult education.

National Literacy Mission

National Literacy Mission was launched on 5th May, 1988 to equip all citizens of the country with functional literacy. In quantitative terms, the mission seeks to impart functional literacy to 80 million illiterate persons in the 15-35 years age group by the end of 1995. National Literacy Mission is extended upto 2010. In quantitative terms, functional literacy implies: (*a*) Self-reliance in 3 R's; (*b*) Participation in development process; (*c*) Providing skills to improve economic status and general well-being; and (*d*) Imbibing values of national integration, conservation of environment, women's equality and observance of small family norms etc., National Literacy Mission lays major emphasis on rural areas, particularly women and persons belonging to scheduled castes and scheduled tribes who constitute the majority of the illiterate segments. Further, NLM aims at:

- Involving voluntary agencies in a big way in the task of achieving literacy and other programmes of continuing education;
- Providing facilities for post-literacy and continuing education and short duration vocational training courses through the establishment of Jana Shikshana Nilayams (JSNs);
- Strengthening and improving the status of the ongoing adult education programmes *viz*., Rural

Functional Literacy Programmes, Programmes of Shramik Vidyapeeths and voluntary agencies with the application of science and technology inputs, better supervision, suitable training, pedagogical innovations etc.;

- Restarting of functional literacy programmes for women as an integral part of Integrated Child Development Scheme;
- Making systematic efforts to secure people's participation through media and communication, creation of local participatory structure, taking out of jathas, mass rallies and training of cadres of youth;
- Undertaking technology demonstration in 40 districts for development, transfer and application of techno-pedagogic inputs;
- Reducing the span of control of supervision from 30 adult education centres to 8-10 adult education centres. The supervisor will be known as Prerak (motivator) and he/she will organize post-literacy and continuing education programmes through Jana Shikshana Nilayams (JSNs).

Total Literacy Campaigns

With the introduction of total literacy campaigns (1989-90 onwards), under National Literacy Mission, the literacy scenario in India has undergone a notable change totally deviating from the traditional approaches and radical changes were made in the implementation strategies of literacy programme, the dominant strategy being the campaign approach. The campaign is based on area specific, time bound, volunteer-based and cost effective approaches. Through this new approach more than two-thirds of the districts in India have been covered by total literacy campaigns in a short period of five years. Among these, majority of the districts have already progressed from basic literacy phase to post-literacy phase and many are now on the threshold of third phase i.e., continuing education. With this, a situation is fast emerging whereby millions of illiterates are acquiring basic literacy skills and joining the class of neo-literates each year. Without a meaningful scheme of post-literacy and continuing education many of these persons may relapse into the old world of illiteracy. The earlier experience in the field of adult education in India, and that of several other countries, is an ample testimony to this fact. Kerala paved the way for total literacy campaigns and a good majority of the districts followed the campaign approach. Post-literacy aspects were given equal weightage as that of literacy in the total literacy campaigns.

Post-literacy and Continuing Education

Relapse into illiteracy is a serious problem in adult education. This is due to lack of adequate usage of the limited skills acquired by the learners in their daily lives. The learners who attend the literacy programme for a shorter duration and pay less care to retain literacy skills will be relapsing into illiteracy. It is necessary to cultivate and continue reading and writing on their part so that the initial achievement may not be lost in course of time. This requires development of proper reading materials for the neo-literates and sufficient practice of literacy skills acquired by learners in varied domains of life. The materials may include simple posters, pictures, folders, pamphlets, books, periodicals, newsletters, etc.

Continuing education is a process of leaning that continues throughout life. Continuing education facilities have to be provided on a permanent basis. The main aim of continuing education programme is to ensure that a comprehensive range of appropriate opportunities are available for life long learning. In operational terms, continuing education includes post-literacy skills, continuing learning beyond elementary literacy and application of this learning for improving their living conditions. Continuing education includes all of the learning opportunities people want or need outside the basic literacy education and primary education. In continuing education, human resource development becomes the focus of attention. The beneficiaries of continuing education programmes are: neo-literates of total literacy campaigns, pass-outs of non-formal education, primary schools, school dropouts and other members of the community interested in life-long learning.

Objectives

The main objectives of the scheme and the activities taken up under continuing education include the following:

- Provision of facilities for retention of literacy skills and continuing education to enable the learners to continue their learning beyond basic literacy;
- Creating scope for application of functional literacy for improvement of living conditions and quality of life;
- Dissemination of information on development programmes and widening and improving participation of traditionally deprived sections of the society;
- Creation of awareness about national concerns such as national integration, conservation and improvement of the environment, women's equality, observance of small family norms, etc., and sharing of common problems of the community;
- Improvement of economic conditions and general wellbeing as well as improvement of productivity by organizing short duration training programmes, orientation courses for providing vocational skills and by taking up linkage activities for establishing direct linkage between continuing education and development activities;

- Provision of facilities for library and reading rooms for creating an environment conducive for literacy efforts and a learning society;
- Organization of cultural and recreational activities with effective community participation.

Functions of Continuing Education Centres

As mentioned above, the main objective of establishment of CECs is to serve as a window or a local service point where diverse kinds of Continuing Education Programmes and activities are taken up to provide opportunities for life-long learning to all section of the population. The functions of CEC would include:

- *Organisation of evening classes*: for the upgradation and acquisition of different skills like literacy. Classes will be organized for 3-4 hours once in a week;
- *Provision of Library and reading facilities*: for which books would be purchased from the non-recurring and recurring provisions; copies of old journals will be maintained and useful booklets relating to development programmes will be published by the agencies concerned. Wall papers and newspapers, appropriate for adult learners, informative and entertaining journals, developmental literature etc., would also be available;
- *A Charcha Mandal (Discussion Group):* for discussion on common problems. This forum could be utilized for improvement of quality of life and individual interest programmes;
- *Training Programmes*: simple and short duration programmes relating to such subjects as health and family welfare, new developments in agriculture and animal husbandry, conservation of energy, improved chulha, etc. CECs may also help the local youth to

benefit from various vocational training programmes, income generation programmes, which help participants acquire or upgrade vocational skills and enable them to conduct income generating activities, should be made available in structured packages;

- *Sports and adventurous activities*: the stress being on indigenous sports, walking excursions, cycling trips in group, etc. If savings are available, visit by bus to development projects could also be arranged;
- *Recreational and cultural activities*: particularly traditional and folk forms of art, rural theatre, puppetry, etc.;
- *An Information window*: for securing information on various developmental programmes. Information and material suitable for neo-literates may be procured from the development agencies concerned;
- *A communication centre*: where community radio, audio cassettes player-cum-recorder may be provided.

Jana Shikshan Sansthan

The first Shramik Vidyapeeth was established in Mumbai in the year 1967 and gradually the number increased to 17 upto 1883 and to 58 by the end of VIII five year plan *i.e.*, 1996-97. Later, the scheme of Shramik Vidyapeeth has been renamed as Jana Shikshan Sansthan (JSS)-Institute of People's Education. Under the new scheme 33 more JSS were sanctioned and the number is increased to 91 by the end of October 2000. These institutions have already proved to be one of the best vocational adult education centres in the country and the courses offered by those institutions are in popular demand. Now, JSSs offer around 225 different types of vocational training programmes ranging from papad making to computers. Men and women belonging mostly to the unorganized sector living in urban and rural areas and people who had been migrating from rural to urban settings are expected to derive benefits from this scheme. The Jan Sikshan Sansthans are expected to adopt continuing education centres and organize academic courses and income generating programmes for the benefit of neo-literates.

Profile of Chittoor District

It is necessary to understand the profile of the district and its social, physical and educational aspects in order to design effective strategies for adult education activities. Chittoor District was constituted on 1st April, 1911, comprising the Taluks of Chittoor, Palamaner, and Chandragiri transferred from North Arcot district of Tamil Nadu, Madanapalle and Voyalpadu Taluks from Kadapa District and Ex-Zamindari areas of Punganur, Srikalahasthi, Puttur and Old Karvetinagar Easter by 1.12.1928 Kangundhi Taluk of North Arcot District, with the exception of 22 Villages was transferred to Palamaner Taluk and in 1950 under the province and States (Absorption of Enclaves) Order, 8 Villages of Mysore State were transferred to Palamaner Taluk. The next major change in Jurisdiction of the District took place on 1st April 1960 as a result of Pataskar Award. Consequent on the re-organisation of the state on linguistic basis, a major portion of Thiruthani Taluk was Transferred to Chengalpattu district of Tamil Nadu. Instead One Taluk Known as Sathyavedu comprising 76 villages of Tiruvallur Taluk, 72 villages of Ponneri Taluk, both of Changalpattu District of Tamil Nadu and 17 villages of Puttur Taluk, 19 villages of Thirthani Taluk was constituted and added to Chittoor district. Also from the same date, the Sub Taluks of Kuppam and Bangarupalem were constituted transferring 220 villages from Palamaner Taluk and 3 villages from Krishnagiri Taluk of Selam District of Tamil Nadu to form Kuppam Sub-taluk and 145 Villages from Chittoor Taluk to form Bangarupalem sub-taluk. Subsequently Kuppam and Bangarupalem were made full-fledged Taluks. The above 11

Taluks of the District were re-organised into 15 Taluks and 20 Panchayath Samithis. Again the above 15 Taluks of the District were re-organised into 66 Revenue Mandals as per G.O. Ms.No.569-Revenue (Mandal-2) Dept., Dt: 22.05.1985.

Boundaries and Topography

The district is bound on the North by Anantapur and Kadapa District, on the East by Nellore District and Chengalpattu District of Tamil Nadu. On the South by North Arcot District of Tamil Nadu and on the west by Tamil Nadu and Karnataka States. The District covers an extent of 15,152 Sq.Kms. It is divided into 3 Revenue Divisions *viz.*, Chittoor, Tirupati and Madanapalle. It is situated between 12° - 37", 14° - 8" of North latitude and 78° - 33" to 79° - 55" of the Eastern Longitude.

The District can be divided in to two natural divisions:

1. The Mountainous Plateau on the West comprising the 31 Mandals of Madanapalle Division;
2. The plains on the East comprising the Mandals of Puttur, Narayanavanam, Vadamalpet, Kammapalle, Karvetinagar, Vedurukuppam, S.R. Puram, Palasamudram, Nagari, Nindra, Vijayapuram, Pitchatur, Nagalapuram, Sathyavedu, Varadaiahpalem, B.N. Kandriga, Kovanur, Thottambedu, Srikalahasthi and Yerpedu. The Mandals viz., Chittoor, G.D. Nellore, Puthalapattu, Penumur, Gudipala, Yadamari, Thavanampalle and Irala stand almost as dividing line between the two natural divisions of the District. The eastern ghats are predominant in the western region and they gradually bend towards the scared hills of Tirupati, passing through Chandagiri erstwhile taluk and entering into Nellore District. The general elevation of the mountainous part of the district is 2500 ft., above sea level.

Climate

The Climate of the District is dry and healthy. The upland mandals consist of 31 Mandals in Mandanapalle Division are comparatively cooler than the eastern Mandals except Chittoor where the climate is moderate.

Rainfall

The district has the benefit of receiving rainfall during both the South West and North East Monsoon periods. While the normal rainfall of the District for the South West Monsoon period is 438.00 MMs that for North east Monsoon period is 396.00 MMs. The rainfall received during the winter period and hot weather period is negligible, their respective normals being 12.0 MMs and 88.0 MMs. The annual normal rainfall of the District is 934.0 MMs. The rainfall received from the South West Monsoon is more copious compared to North East Monsoon in the Western Mandals and in the Central part of the District, where as the rainfall received from North East Monsoon is comparatively copious in the eastern Mandals of the District.

Rivers

The rivers flowing in the District are non-perennial in nature in that they remain dry for a major part of the year. Of these rivers, river Ponnai which is tributary of river Palar rises in erst-while Chittoor Taluk and flowing towards the South, joins the Palar in Tamil Nadu. The Swarnamukhi another important river which rises in the eastern ghats in erst-while Chandaragiri Taluk has its course through out the mandals of erst-while Chandragiri Taluk and part of erst-while Srikalhasthi Taluk and ultimately flows into Nellore District. Other such important rivers of the District are Kusastali, Bheema, Bahuda, the Pincha, the Kalyani, Araniyar and Pedderu which flow in different Mandals of the District. Besides the above rivers, there are a number of small hilly streams flowing in the District.

Soils

The Major portion of the District is covered by red soils with portions of the Alluvial soil in Chittoor and Bangarupalem erst-while Taluks. According to an assessment made on the basis of Village records, 57 per cent of the soils of the district are loamy and 34 per cent Red Sandy. The remaining 9 per cent is covered by black clay (3 per cent) Black loamy (2 per cent Black) Sandy (1 per cent) and Red clay (3 per cent).

Minerals

The District is not rich in mineral wealth, steatite is the only mineral mined in Puttur and G.D.Nellore erst-while block areas of the District. However, the occurrence of gold, iron and red moulding sand are also noticed in certain parts of the District. In Bisanatham area of Kuppam erst-while taluk, the Auriferous veins are 22 per cent wide and carry an average gold content of 5.190-wts. of gold per tonne. Iron ore occurred in Voyalpadu, Srikalahasthi and Puttur erstwhile taluks.

Irrigation

There are 8 medium Irrigation Projects in the District. They are Swarnamukhi, Araniyar, Mallimadugu, Kalangi, Bahuda, Siddalagandi Project, Krishnapuram Reservoir and Pedderu Project. The total registered ayacut under the eight projects is 15310 Hectares.

There are 7512 minor irrigation tanks with a total ayacut of 54,336.14 Hectares. The District occupies a pride of place in the number of irrigation wells totaling to 1,16,239 in number. Comparison of the district with state of different aspects, population and literacy in the district (1901-2001) total and mandal-wise are appended.

Literacy Activities in Chittoor District

Chittoor is the first district in Andhra Pradesh and third district in the country to take up total literacy campaign. The first one is Ernakulam in Kerala and the second one is Burdwan in West Bengal. Chittoor district is situated in the southern part of Andhra Pradesh with Tamil Nadu and Karnataka on either side. Telugu is the dominant language of Chittoor, which is also influenced by Tamil and Kannada. The district is known as a holy district due to the existence of temples at Tirumala, Tiruchanoor and Srikalahasti. The total literacy campaign was formally launched on 2nd October, 1990 with a lot of commitment, zeal and enthusiasm by Zilla Saksharatha Samaithi, Chittoor.

'Akshara Tapasman' was the name of the total literacy campaign of Chittoor district. It is interesting to note as to why it was named after Tapasman. The term 'Tapasman' is the traditional term rooted in the folk lore of Chittoor district. The origin of the tradition related to an episode in Mahabharata, wherein 'Arjuna' is supposed to have done 'Tapas' and acquired the divine weapon 'Pasupatastra' which helped him to win the Kurukshetra war. Arjuna did Tapas with all his attention and concentration and did not stop till he succeeded in his effort. The same level of attention and concentration is necessary on the part of an illiterate person suffering from poverty, exploitation, and ignorance. The day to day life of a common man is a 'battle'. 'Literacy' and 'Awareness' are the two most potent weapons to fight this 'battle'. The 'Tapas' started with an aim to provide the weapons of literacy and awareness to help the illiterate poor to overcome their predicaments. The campaign aimed at the age group of 9-35 and 6 lakh illiterate persons were enrolled in the literacy centres throughout the district. An external evaluation conducted by the Osmania University, Hyderabad (1991) revealed that 86.7 per cent of literacy was achieved by implementing the campaign in the district among the target group of 9-35 years.

Strengths of the Campaign

District Collector's commitment (Sri Nagarjuna) was a

highlight of the campaign. He worked relentlessly in planning and implementing the various aspects of the campaign., such as constitution of various committees (academic, cultural, monitoring, evaluation etc.), guiding literacy workers, facilitating finalization of primers for approval by National Literacy Mission Authority, reducing the time gap in various facets of the campaign, delegating authority and responsibility to mandal level officers and co-ordinators, securing the support of the press for popularising the campaign, maintaining round the clock office for literacy work, training, monitoring etc.

The involvement of the educational institutions was another significant issue to be considered. Literacy work became the prime concern for the school teachers from the beginning and the teachers worked as mandal co-ordinators, village co-ordinators and as promoters of literacy.

The untiring efforts of sixty thousands volunteers representing various parts of the district to teach learners was another remarkable aspect of the campaign. Participation of the students and educated members especially in the villages in the campaign became a question of pride, courage, concern and respect for them.

The usage of local art forms like harikatha, burrakatha, jakki, pandari bhajana, chekka bhajana, pulivesham, pillamgrovi, kolatam widened the scope of the campaign by touching the nook and corners of the villages.

The visits made by the district and mandal level administrators including the collector, district development officer and others motivated the learners and educated members to participate in the campaign. The campaign was viewed as a people's campaign in which all sections of the society involved themselves voluntarily and contributed their level best for its success. The involvement of development departments like revenue, agriculture and animal husbandary gave more impetus for the campaign. With regard to the involvement of voluntary agencies the role played by Bharatha Gyana Vignana Samithi (BGVS) was commendable especially in environment building.

The campaign laid more stress on creating awareness of right for land, rainfed agriculture, women's emancipation, minimum wages, evil effects of consumption of alcohol, immunization, equality of opportunities, co-operation, education, untouchability etc. The non-acceptance of thumb impression by government officials created more demand for literacy. Attendance in literacy centres was made a minimum requirement, unofficially, for issue of ration items and this helped to ensure regular participation of learners in the centres.

The organization of door to door campaigns, padayatras, processions, personal contacts with volunteers, periodical meetings, review meetings of co-ordinators and literacy activists, celebration of literacy festivals, literacy conventions, literacy week (Akshara Saptaham), motivation campaigns, volunteer exchange programmes, issue of shoulder bags, identity cards, distribution of leaflets/folders about the campaign helped a lot for its better implementation. Among other things, wall writings, banners, cabsters, puppet shows, cinema slides, use of vans with audio cassettes, public meetings, essay writing and elocution competitions at schools and colleges were notable. The involvement of youth clubs, mahila mandals, Nehru Yuvak Kendras, District Institute of Education and Training, ex-service men, writers etc, has given sufficient support for the campaign. After the completion of total literacy campaign in a successful manner, the district has initiated 10,000 Jana Chaithanya Kendras (JCKs) for the purpose of post-literacy activities. The JCKs were continued upto 1996 and continuing education centres were initiated from 1997 onwards.

In order to cover the left avers, dropouts and nearly attained age group who are remaining non-literate, the district has taken up different programmes and the preraks at the village level were entrusted with the responsibility of implementing the programmes. The details are as follows:

Table 1.2 : Literacy Activities in Chittoor District (2001-2006)

Year	Name of the Programme	No. of learners Enrolled made literate		% of success
2000 -01	Akshara Sankranthi Phase I	172555	112504	65.20
2001-02	Akshara Sankranthi Phase II	74149	55772	75.22
2002-03	Akshara Sankranthi Phase III	46989	37942	80.75
2003-04	Akshara Sankranthi Phase IV	808440	69936	86.94
2004-05	Akshara Bharathi Phase I	139070	118875	85.48
2005-06	Akshara Bharathi Phase II	41998	32173	76.42
Total		**555191**	**427202**	

The above table indicates that the district has implemented 4 phases of Akshara Sankranthi Programme and 2 phases of Akshara Bharathi Programme. Still there are 1,27,989 non-literates to be covered. The district has started Bapuji Vignana Kendras (BVKs) in selected community education centres at panchayat level in order to extend the facilities of open schooling, library and continuing education activities. Income generating activities are carried out in the BVKs with the support of voluntary agencies and Jana Sikshana Samsthan (JSS) located at Tirupati. As many as 298 continuing education centres in Chittoor revenue division, 208 continuing education centres in Tirupati revenue division, and 500 continuing education centres in Madanapalli, 143 nodal continuing education centres are functioning in the district. The literacy percentage of the district as per 2001 centres is 67.46 per cent. Among men it is 78.29 and among women the literacy rate is 56.48 per cent.

The Present Study

The Government of India has accorded top priority for adult education programmes after independence as a result of which the literacy rate has been improving decade by decade. However, the problem of basic literacy is continuing. It is necessary to know the extent to which the neo-literates emerging out of various programmes are able to retain the literacy levels and to know the influence of various personal, social, economic and psychological factors on their achievement in order to suggest workable solutions. The review presented in Chapter II revealed that not many studies have been conducted on the achievement/performance of learners/neo-literates in relation to personal, social, economic and psychological factors. Though a good number of the evaluations on total literacy/post-literacy campaign were taken up by different agencies yet they were limited to indicating the achievement of learners at the district, mandal, panchayat levels for the purpose of financial requirements for future programmes *i.e.,* post-literacy and continuing education. In the case of Chittoor district, the task of covering the illiterates, dropouts and the newly attained age groups is given to the preraks and it is one of their essential functions. In some mandals the community members are actively participating and in some mandals they are participating at poor and moderate levels. The level of participation of neo-literates in the continuing education centres is also not uniform. Hence attention is needed on measures relating to enhancing the achievement level of neo-literates. The present study is an ardent effort in this direction.

An Overview of Succeeding Chapters

In the *second chapter,* the Review Related Literature is presented. *Chapter three* deals with Statement of the Problem, Objectives and Hypotheses whereas *chapter four* concentrates on Methodology of Investigation. In *chapter Five,* Analysis of Results is presented. *Chapter Six* deals with Summary and conclusions, Suggestions for Further Research and Implications of the study.

2

Review of Related Literature

The review of related literature is an important aspect in any research. Each new generation of human beings makes use of accumulated knowledge as a foundation for building up further knowledge. Hence, the study of literature is necessary in any field of enquiry. In the field of adult education as in other fields too, the researcher needs to acquire up-to-date information about the area of research. It helps the investigator to decide whether the evidence already available solves the problem adequately without further investigation, and thus to avoid risk of duplication. The literature provides ideas, theories explanation etc., valuable in formulating the problems and methods of research appropriate to it. A careful review of the research journals, books, dissertations and other sources of information on the problems to be investigated are one of the important steps in planning of any research work. Further, study of the related literature allows the researcher to acquaint himself with current knowledge in the field or area in which he is going to conduct research. The study of related literature enables the researcher to define the limits of his/her field. Review of related literature widens knowledge, deepens understanding and builds up ideas and insights for better perspective and therefore is an essential aspect of research. The availability and utilization of adequate sources of related information are essential for a proper research activity. It gives adequate information about different researches related to the present study. It also guides and directs the researcher to collect useful material for the purpose of study. It locates comparative data and findings useful in the interpretation and discussion of results. It helps in developing expertise and general scholarship of the investigator in the area investigated.

The role of research is vital in suggesting solutions to the field level problems. Bhola (1967) rightly feels that a professional area like adult education needs not only researchers and research studies but also a research tradition. Draper (1973) feels that much research needs to be done on adult education in India with reference to backward communities and on the field level problems. One of the import areas of research in adult education is related to the participation of adult learners in the centres. How adults learn? What are the factor influencing their participation and achievement in the centres? Questions of this nature need to be answered by the researchers and empirical evidences need to be added to the stock of research works done on adult learners. The effective utilisation of the results to strengthen the field programmes requires the attention of the field level practitioners in adult education. The review of related literature is presented in this chapter.

Studies on Personal, Social and Economic Factors *(Gender, Age, Caste, Occupation, Marital Status, Income)*

Reporting on investigation carried out by Literacy House, Lucknow, Ahmed (1958) said, "Women were found to do better than men in acquisition of literacy skills. 25 per cent of men failed in the test, whereas only 17 per cent of the women failed to qualify. 58 per cent of the men were good at reading a comprehension, whereas 64.5 per cent of the women qualified as good readers, on an average, women completed the primer in 2.21 months well below the 3.12 months average of the total population.

The studies conducted by Directorate of Adult Education (1973) and Pillai (1976) on participants of farmers Functional Literacy denoted that learners of lower age group fared better in literacy tests as compared to those of older age group.

Simmons (1972) observed that the age of the participants had not influence on their academic achievement. Prakesh (1978) found that learning of adults had little relationship to their ages. Reddy (1980) also reported that no significant differences existed between younger and older age group learners in their learning ability.

Hebsur Aikara and Herniques (1981) in their second evaluation report on National Adult Education Programme in Maharashtra indicated that the performance of women and persons from lower castes was poorer than that of other groups.

Pabitra and others (1993) through their evaluation study found that the performance of the minority groups and scheduled castes was good in terms of overall attainment of literacy. Venkataiah (1977) through his study on learners attending Farmers Functional Literacy Programme in Andhra Pradesh found that the age of the participants was inversely related to the acquisition of literacy skills. He found that higher castes group had acquired literacy skills better than the learners representing lower castes.

Khajapeer (1978) through his study on academic performance of Farmers Functional Literacy Programme participants reported that sex, age and caste of the participants had no relationship to their academic performance.

The evaluation study conducted by Bikaner Adult Education Association (1973) showed that women were little better than men in acquisition of literacy skills. Mathur (1976) in his evaluation study also found that women were slightly better than men in learning 3 R's. Naik (1979) in his quick appraisal of National Adult Education Programme in Gujarat also indicated that female learners had an edge over male learners in learning literacy skills. Salamatullah and Bareth (1984) in their evaluation report noted that the performance of women in literacy attainment was found to be better than that of men.

Tribhuvan University (1982) undertook a study with the following objectives: To determine the participants' achievement level of literacy (reading, writing and numeracy). To make a comparative study of the achievement patters of participants on the basis of their difference in sex, language and geographical location and to examine to what extent the programmes regarding agriculture, health, sanitation, and social welfare were assimilated by the participants. The study shed light on the following facts: 60 percent of the participants of Functional Adult Education Programme became literate. No significant differences were found in the achievements of male and female adults in literacy. Around 90 percent of the adults acquired sufficient knowledge about social reforms, health and hygiene from the literacy classes.

Pestonjee, Laharia and Dixit (1981) in their second appraisal of National Adult Education programme in Rajasthan found that men were better than women in achievement of literacy skills. Mariappan, Suseela and Ramakrishna (1981) in their evaluation study of National Adult Education Programme in Pondicherry reported that men were better achievers than women with regard to literacy, functional development and social awareness. Grewal (1992) conducted a study on Adult Education Programme in Madhya Pradesh State. The finding of the study revealed that males were better learners on the various components of literacy than the females in all the four clusters.

Burdwan Zilla Saksharata Samiti (1991) brought a publication consisting the reports of the external evaluation of the "Total literacy campaign of Burdwan district'. The external evaluation of Burdwan district was conducted by an expert committee consisting of social scientists like Mohit Bhattacharya, A.K.Jalaluddin, Satyan Maitra and Mustaq Ahmed. The findings of the evaluation report are as follows: Majority of the learners had acquired considerable speed in literacy as laid down in the NLM norm. There is a wide range of difference between the learning abilities of adult learners, which is usually the case. Among the different groups of learners, Muslim learners showed the best results; 93.0 percent reached the norm and 80.0 percent came in the excellent category. Similarly the scheduled castes fared much better as compared to scheduled tribes and others. The main reason for the tribals showing slightly lower results than other groups, appeared to be language difficulty. There was no apparent difference between the males and females in the literacy activity. However, a higher percentage of the males reached excellent levels.

Mustaq Ahmed and others (1992) conducted an evaluation on Total Literacy Campaign of Midnapore District (West Bengal). The report showed that total literacy campaign in Midnapore was approved by National Literacy Mission Authority in July 6th, 1990 and campaign ended in the month of March 1992. Evaluation was carried out on 19,899 learners representing, 7 sub-divisions, 54 blocks, and 11 urban units in Midnapore District. The test was conducted according to NLM norms. A minimum of 50 percent marks each in reading, writing and arithmetic were required and 70 percent in aggregate was kept as the cut off point for ascertaining the number of literates. The findings of the study were as follows: Out of 19,899 learners, 75 percent obtained 50 percent or more scores in reading, writing, and numeracy skills separately and 60 per cent or more in aggregate. Thus 77.60 percent learners were found to have attained the NLM norms. The campaign was uniformly successful throughout the district. Relatively speaking, numeracy skills of learners were most developed and writing skills were weakest. Performance of learners in rural areas was found to be much better as compared to the urban areas. The coverage of illiterates from the minority and tribes has also been less satisfactory as compared to other communities. Adult learners performed better than non-formal education group learners. Within the adult age group, the performance of the learners aged above 35 was inferior to that of others. Performance of male learners was better than that of female learners. Learners with some previous formal schooling background, even if rudimentary, performed slightly better than those who never attended any formal school. Improved Pace and Content of Learning (IPCL) primer appeared to be more effective than the general primer.

Ramachandra (1994) conducted a study on "Reading Proficiency of Learners in the Total Literacy Campaign of Chinnagottigallu Mandal". The findings of the study are as follows: (1) There was a significant difference between males and females in the mean performance of reading proficiency and the performance of male learners was good; (2) There was no significant difference between the younger age group and the older age group in the mean performance of reading proficiency; (3) Marital status of the learners had no significant influence on their reading proficiency; (4) There was significant relationship between the caste of the learners and their performance in reading. The performance of learners who belonged to the backward castes and scheduled castes/ scheduled tribes was lower when compared to the performance of those who belonged to forward castes; (5) There was a significant relationship between the reading proficiency of learners and their family income. Learners belonging to higher income groups performed better than the learners from lower income groups; (6) There existed a significant relationship between occupation of learners and their performance in reading proficiency. The performance of non-agricultural group was better than the learners of agricultural group; (7) There was significant relationship between the reading proficiency of learners and the availability of physical facilities in the centres. Learners who belonged to centres where adequate material facilities were available performed better than those who belonged to centres where the physical facilities were poor; (8) There was significant positive relationship between reading proficiency of learners and the help and encouragement given by their family members, relatives, friends and community leaders. Learners who had better community support scored better than those who had less community support in their performance in reading; and (9) Regression analysis, considering adult learners performance on 'Reading test as the source of variance, indicated that factors namely, attitude, sex and material factors had significant impact on their proficiency and accounted for 53.32 per cent of variance.

Vasudeva Rao (1988) found that male sex, younger age, un-married social status, joint family background, rural nativity, higher income and regular attendance helped the adult learners to gain more skills in literacy, and to raise their functionality and awareness. The caste and occupation of the learners had a little impact, compared to the other socio-economic variables.

Tata Institute of Social Sciences (1993) evaluated Total Literacy Campaign in Lathur. About 82 per cent of the evaluated learners scored above 50 per cent marks in the literacy test as per the external evaluation test norms and 49.7 per cent as per the national literacy norms, 58.4 per cent of the males, 45.2 per cent of females, 51.6 per cent of the learners in rural areas and 38.95 per cent of the learners in the urban areas achieved success in the test. The success of scheduled castes and scheduled tribes is better in relation to others. It was found that the mean performance is good in numeracy than in reading and writing.

Sardar Patel Institute of Economic and Social Research (1994) evaluated the literacy campaign of Dang district of Gujarath. The findings of the study showed that 62 per cent of the sample learners secured 50 per cent of marks in aggregate and only 23.93 per cent secured 70 per cent marks in aggregate. The out come of male learners is better than that of the females. Occupation wise 80 per cent labourers have secured more than 50 per cent of the marks in relation to others.

Denzil Saldhana's (1992) found that a good majority of adult learners enrolled in the total literacy campaign were in the 15-35 years age group and their performance in literacy skills was also good in relation to 36 and above age group.

Kulasekhar (2005) conducted a study on the factors influencing performance of scheduled tribe learners. The sample of study consisted of 280 scheduled tribe learners randomly selected from 7 mandals of Chittoor district. (Renigunta, Yerpedu, Puttur, Chandragiri, Srikalahasthi, Nagalapuram and Satyavedu). About 42.86 per cent of the sample have obtained literacy skills as per norms. It was found that gender, age, marital status and income have significantly influenced the performance of scheduled tribe learners. Further, occupation has not significantly influenced the performance of learners. The trend of the mean scores indicated that women had an edge over men learners. The performance of higher age (35 years and above) was found to be better in relation to the lower age groups. Out of different occupational groups the performance of learners pursuing agriculture was better in relation to learners pursuing other occupations like casual workers, livestock rearing, shepherd, fishing and forest product collection. The performance of married group of learners and higher income groups was found to be better in relation to their counterparts.

Rajendrudu (2005) conducted a study on the performance of adult learners. The sample of the study consisted of 90 adult learners. The result of the study revealed out of 90 members only 21 members constituting 23.33 per cent of the samples have qualified in the literacy test as per NLM norms (50 per cent of marks in reading, writing and numeracy and 70 per cent on aggregate). Better achievement scores are obtained by the sample in reading test followed by writing and numeracy. The performance scores of learners in reading, writing, numeracy and total achievement are more or less normally distributed. The mean achievement scores of learners in reading, writing, numeracy and total achievement are 23.50, 16.40, 14.33 and 53.33 respectively. Gender has significantly influenced the performance of learners. Women learners have obtained a better mean performance score in relation to men learners in reading, writing, numeracy and total achievement. Age has significantly influenced the performance of learners in numeracy and total achievement. The mean performance scores of learners representing below 30 years age group were better than the learners representing 30 years and above age group. Caste has significantly influenced the performance of learners in case of reading, numeracy and total achievement. The mean achievement scores of learners representing forward castes were better than those of backward castes, scheduled castes and scheduled tribes in literacy skills. Occupation has not significantly influenced the performance of learners. The trend of the mean performance scores revealed that the learners belonging to agricultural occupation have scored better means in relation to others (coolies, potters, weavers, etc.) in reading, writing, numeracy and total achievement. Marital has significantly influenced the performance of learners. The married group of learners have scored better means in reading, writing, numeracy and total achievement in relation to the unmarried group.

Institute for Development Research and Alternatives (2001) conducted Evaluation of Akshara Sankrathi programme in Khamam district, Andhra Pradesh. The sample of study consisted 4782 learners. The results of study revealed that the performance of women was better than that of men. The learners below 20 years performed better than 21 to 40 years and 41 years and above. The performance of forward castes was the highest duly followed by backward castes, scheduled castes and scheduled tribes. The occupation wise distribution in literacy attainment showed that the performance of learners belonging to petty business, skill works etc. was better then the learners belonging to agriculture and labour groups.

Kumaraswamy, *et al.* (2007) conducted external evaluation Akshara Bharathi Phase II of Medak District, Andhra Pradesh, For the purpose of the study a sample 3635 adult learners who completed their literacy course were selected. An evaluation tool was developed to assess the performance of adult learners in literacy skills as per National Literacy Mission norms. The overall achievement of literacy as per the evaluation was 46.96 per cent. Results revealed that the performance of women was better than men, the performance 15-35 years age group was better than 36 years above age group and the performance of backward castes was better than forward castes, scheduled castes, and scheduled tribes in literacy attainment.

Shankar (1972) conducted an experiment to find out literacy attainments of two groups of adult literacy class participants: (1) participants in the classes conducted for a period of six months strictly according to the time schedule to finish the functional literacy courses; and (2) participants in the classes conducted over an extended period of nine months to finish the same functional literacy course and the average literacy attainments of these two course were compared. The findings of the study were: (1) the average writing speed per minute after nine months was more by 14 words than the average writing speed after six months; (2) Surprisingly, the average reading speed per minute was less by 24 words after nine months than what it was after six months. From these findings, it was concluded that when the six months course was prolonged and spread over nine months: (1) there was no improvement in reading speed but; (2) the writing speed improved.

Nanda and Beri (1974) undertook an investigation into the perception of the advantage of the literacy programme by the adults attending adult literacy centers in Patiala Circle. The sample includes both men and women. The study revealed that the biggest advantage of literacy as perceived by the adults was acquisition of reading skills (86 per cent male, 75 per cent females). The other advantages in attaining literacy in the literacy centers as perceived by the adults include increase in knowledge (58.5%) help in sewing and embroidery (95% among female), help in attaining further education (44%), help in agricultural production (36.5%) and help in domestic affairs (31% among females). Further, the sample indicated that adult literacy attained by other adults earlier had proved useful in the following areas – reading (66%), keeping accounts (11%) writing letters (7%), help in domestic affairs (5%), help in agriculture production (3%), knowledge about country (1%) and knowledge about health and hygiene (1%).

Rao (1983) made a comparative study of relative effectiveness of sentence and alphabetic method. He found that alphabetic method was better than sentence method. Further, within the alphabetic method, teaching/ reading for the first two months followed by writing was found more effective than the conventional alphabetic method in which reading and writing were done simultaneously.

Indra Deva and Others (1992) evaluated the total literacy campaign of Narasingapur, West Bengal. With respect to performance of learners, it was found that majority of the learners were weak in recognizing letters and letters of not frequent occurrence. The performance of men was higher than that of women in the centres. The main reason for low levels of achievement in literacy was found to be learners failure to qualify in the writing ability. Only half of the sample of learners could attain the literacy levels as per NLM norms. Self-writing was not at all developed. That is why most of the learners secured very poor marks in letter writing and writing of address.

Sardar Patel Institute of Economic and Social Research (1994) evaluated the literacy campaign of Sundar Nagar District. The study showed that more than 86 per cent of the neo-literates scored 50 per cent marks, while 22 per cent secured 70 per cent and above marks in literacy test. The achievement in reading, writing and numeracy is found to be 83 per cent, 62 per cent and 88 per cent respectively.

Sudhakar Reddy *et.al.* (1997) conducted external evaluation of total literacy campaign, Chitrdurga district, Karnataka state. For the purpose of the evaluation, four types of subjects namely: (*a*) neo-literates, (*b*) volunteers, (*c*) community leaders; and (*d*) functionaries were chosen. The sample of neo-literates was finalized with the assistance of District/ Taluk authorities associated with the campaign. Out of the 1,96,860 neo-literates (who had completed primer III) available in the district, 12,820 neo-literates were chosen. Ample care was taken in the selection of the sample to give due representation to all categories of the target population. With respect to volunteer and community leaders one volunteers and one community leader from each village represented by the sample neo-literates were chosen as subjects. In addition, District, Taluk and Panchayat level functionaries representing the sample neo-literates were chosen as the subjects.

The literacy achievement test and the questionnaires were administered to the respective target samples. The Literacy test was administered to the neo-literates by investigators chosen, trained and appointed for the purpose. They administered the test under the supervision of local coordinators and university representatives. Further, the investigators distributed the respective questionnaires to the volunteers, community leaders and functionaries allotted to the areas and collected the duly filled in questionnaires back from them. Local taluk coordinators assisted in the process. Information obtained through administration of literacy test was translated into numericals and expressed in terms of percentages. In the same way, information collected through the administration of questionnaires to sample volunteers, community leaders and functionaries were analysed. The conclusions drawn through the analysis were as follows:

- The minimum and maximum marks obtained by the neo-literates of the sample were 30 and 95 respectively.
- Less than three percent subjects of the sample scored between 30-39 marks in literacy test.
- About 42 per cent of the total sample represented by 2257 men and 3130 women had scored less than fifty per cent marks in literacy test.
- Marginal differences were noticed in the literacy achievement levels of men and women neo-literates of the sample.
- Nearly seventeen per cent of the sample represented by 959 men and 1209 women neo-literates had scored 50 per cent and above but less than 70 per cent marks in each of the sub-tests of literacy test.
- Nearly fifty per cent of the sample subjects scored 70 per cent and above marks in literacy test (with minimum 50 per cent marks in each sub-test).
- The literacy achievement level of Urdu neo-literates was better than the Kannada neo-literates of the sample.
- Achievement level of urban neo-literates of the sample was better than rural representatives.
- Among the caste groups, poor performance was noticed in the achievement of scheduled tribes neo-literates of the sample.
- The minimum and maximum marks obtained by the neo-literates in reading sub-test were 14 and 39 out of the total 40 marks.

- Majority of the sample subjects had scored low in comprehension unit of reading sub-test.
- The minimum and maximum marks obtained by the sample subjects in writing sub-test were 7 and 28 out of the total 30 marks.
- Good number of subjects of the sample had scored low in letter writing unit of the writing sub-test.
- The minimum and maximum marks obtained by the sample subjects in numeration sub-test were 8 and 30 respectively out of 30 marks.
- Considerable number of the sample subjects appear to have difficulty in solving problems involving divisions followed by problems involving multiplications.

To sum-up, the studies conducted by Ahmad (1958), Bikaneer Adult Education Association(1973), Salamuthullah and Barath (1984), Naik (1979), Mathu (1976), Institute for development Research and Alternatives (2001), have stated that the performance of women is better in acquisition of literacy skills. Contrary to this, the investigations of Hebsur, Aikara, Herniques (1981), Pestonjee, Laharia and Dixit (1981), Mariappan Susheela, Ramakrishna (1981), Grewal (1992), Sardar Patel Institute of Economics and Social Research (1994), Ramachandra (1994) have revealed that the performance of men was better in acquiring the literacy skills. The study conducted by Tribhuvan University (1982) revealed that gender, did not influence the performance of learners in literacy skills.

The researches undertaken by Directorate of Adult Education (1973), Pillai (1976), Institute for Development Research and Alternatives (2001), Mustaq Ahmad and others (1992), Denzil Saldhana (1992) found that the performance of lower age group was better in literacy skills. Simmons (1972), Prakash (1978), Reddy (1980), indicated age had no influence in the acquisition of literacy skills. With respect to caste

Hebsur, Aikara, Herniques (1981), Ramachandra (1994), have found that forward castes have fared well in literacy skills. Khajapeer (1978), Kumaraswamy (1992) have revealed that gender, age and caste do not significantly influence the performance of adult learners in literacy skills. Investigators who have studies performance with a combination of variables gender, age, caste, occupation, marital status have come out with different results. Pabitra and Others (1993) have found that the performance of scheduled castes and minorities was better in literacy skills. Venkataiah (1977) revealed that the performance of lower age group and forward castes was better in literacy skills. The study undertakes Burdwan Zilla Saksharata Samiti (1991) indicated that Muslims fared well than others in literacy test. Tata Institute of Social Sciences (1993) revealed that the performance of scheduled castes and scheduled tribes was better in literacy skills. The study conducted by Ramachandra (1994) on reading achievement indicated that the variables namely age and marital status had no influence on reading achievement. With respect to income and age, Ramachandra (1994) found that higher income group and higher age group have performed well in case of reading achievement. Vasudeva Rao (1980) found that the performance of men, younger age and unmarried was better than their counter parts but caste and occupation had no influence on the literacy of adult learners. Kulasekhar (2005) found that the variables namely gender, age, marital status and income have significantly influenced the performance of scheduled tribes learners and the achievement of learners representing women, higher age, agricultural occupation, married and higher income groups, achievement was better, in literacy skills. Sudhakar Reddy (1997) in his evaluation of Total Literacy Campaign Chitradugra found that the performance of women and forward communities was better in literacy skills. In view of limited number of studies and controversial results on personal factors there is need for further investigations.

Studies on Psychological Factors

Personality of an individual means a particular type of pattern possessed by an individual which is composed of traits or specific qualities of behaviour which characterize an individual's unique adjustment to life as shown in his behaviour and thought. It has long been believed that personality factors are important factors behind the academic achievement of an individual. Based on this belief, certain investigations were conducted to examine the relationship between various personality traits and academic achievement of learners. The investigations conducted varied in this approach based on the aspect and definition of particular facet of personality under investigation. Some of the representative studies were as follows:

Lawton (1951) indicated fear of ridicule, emotional insecurity, feeling of social inadequacy, negative attitude towards learning and uncertainty of future rewards as factors leading to non-participation of adults in learning activity. Roy and Kapoor (1975) after examining the relationship between need achievement of literacy participants and school leavers and their literacy retention reported that n-achievement was a significant factor in literacy retention.

Rama Devi (1962) found that low educated women and non-working women had more traditional values than their counter parts. Khan (1964) found that adults and adolescents from better socio-economic background were less authoritarian than those having lower education or from low socio-economic background. Dellefield (1965) in his study of aspirations observed that adults belonging to low socio-economic status did not feel that education might serve as a medium by which life aspirations could be attained. Singh (1967) found that prevalence of traditional attitude about education was an important cause for illiteracy among adults. Hand and Puder (1968) studied personality correlates interfering with the learning of basic adult education students and found factors like alienation, hostility towards authority, withdrawal and rigid value systems as hindrances to achievement. Jain (1969) found that educational aspirations of heads of households were influenced by a number of factors such as religious affiliation and hierarchy of caste or class to which they belonged.

Sinha (1969) studied the influence of education on the level of aspiration among farmers. Those who had studied upto primary class and higher were included in the educated group and the others in the uneducated group. It was found that the educated from the developed villages tended to aspire significantly higher, had higher positive goal – discrepancy score and showed relatively greater accuracy in estimating their performance. In the under-developed villages, there was no marked difference in the aspirations of educated and uneducated farmers. It was also observed that the educated and illiterate farmers from the developed villages had in comparison to their counterparts from the backward villages significantly higher level of aspiration. Uneducated farmers from under-developed areas also displayed a significant tendency for underestimating their performance. Muthayya (1971) found that literate farmers had higher level of aspiration than illiterate farmers.

Lowe (1975) has listed the following distinct characteristics of adult learners:

- "He is free to avoid, engage in or withdraw from an educational experience as he pleases." Unless what is taught is perceived as either relevant to their life or having potential benefits to them, if not tight away, atleast in the imminent future, he will almost certainly reject it. Also he will discard information and ideas which run counter to his cherished beliefs;
- "He regards the hours that he gives to learning as precious and expects them to be used for some constructive purpose." Unless what is taught is perceived as relevant to their life or having potential

benefits to them, if not right now, at least in the imminent future, he will almost certainly reject it;

- "He usually selects his own area of educational interest and institution through which he will study. And for him, the consequences of learning may well be immediate and far-reaching and therefore he will apply his newly acquired knowledge and skills in his life either at work or in his personal and social life". These have implications on the need for multiplicity of content or problem areas and modes and forms of educational provisions to be identified and evolved that would suit adult learners;
- "The spacing of his learning is directed by his occupational and family commitments and as rule, it will be part-time, irregular, and spread over many years". This has significance for management of adult education because planning and organizing various programmes for adults have to suit their conveniences with regard to time, place and duration;
- "The relationship between the learner and his teacher is very different from that between the pre-adult student and his teacher. The authority of the teacher is determined by competence alone since there can be no question of sanctions, and outside the classroom, adult learners may enjoy higher social and economic status". Since the adult learners and instructors become partners in the learning process, there is parity in their relationship. This also signifies that instructors are in no way superior to adult learners though, within the classroom, the former act as guides and counsellors;
- He holds an image of himself which the teacher must respect;
- There may be no age-gap and the learners' experiences may often exceed that of the teacher;

- Adults are likely to display a cooperative spirit in contrast with the competitiveness of the young; out of their own experience, adult learners can contribute to one another's learning and to a group achievement. This observation signifies how well their cooperative spirit can be cultivated and utilized for action learning and community problem-solving which are unique learning situations present in abundance in the context of adult learning.

Lowe (1975) has also reported invaluable findings relating to learning abilities of adults. Some of the important ones are:

- Intelligence does not automatically decline with age. Studies indicate that the speed of response slows down, the ability to solve problems declines gradually and the motor skills also reduce; but the verbal fluency and comprehension may well increase;
- Adults are not consistently inflexible but vary in their disposition to change according to the nature of tasks set before them;
- Provided that a task is closely formulated and that adults can pace themselves, they perform as well as young people;
- Adults with low level of applied intelligence are more resistant to change than those of higher intelligence;
- The impression that adults cannot learn or that their intelligence deteriorates with age is no more valid for it is an erroneous assumption made by those in authority and also due to negative attitudes adopted towards any new learning;
- There appears to be a particular loss of self-confidence during the later adulthood owing to the cultural conditioning like time, speed and spatial restraints. For instance, adults are normally expected to learn under similar circumstances and conditions

and at the same pace as young people which the former groups find it hard to compete. If adults are allowed to pace themselves, they can learn faster than under constrained and rigid directives.

The above findings are valuable and have greater application for planning and organizing learning experiences for adults. These observations relate mostly to the interactive effects of physical and environmental factors on adult learning. These also point out how maturational decline is counter-balanced by environmental factors. When the mental faculties like speed, perception, reaction, etc., of an aging adult start declining gradually, it is offset by experiences, knowledge and wisdom gained by them.

Khajapeer (1978) while studying the impact of various factors on academic performance of participants attending Farmers Functional Literacy Programme found that academic achievement was positively related to achievement motivation. The investigator also found that persons with conservative out look, fatalistic thinking and authoritarian attitude would be very poor in the attainment of literacy skills.

Reddy (1980) reported that general ability plays a significant role in determining the learning capacity of adults. The investigator found that subjects with high general ability have shown distinctly better learning ability than subjects with low general ability. Swamy (1980), Varalakshmi (1980), and Venkatesulu (1980) through their studies on the relationship of general ability to concept learning tasks among adults found that subjects representing high and how general ability groups of the distribution of Raven's Standard Progressive Matrices test scores differed significantly in their learning abilities.

Lokanadha Reddy (1981) conducted 'a study of certain personality characteristics of active participants and drop-outs enrolled in adult education centres of Sri Kalahasti Project Chittoor District, Andhra Pradesh. The results of the study indicated that the nature of existence of some of the personality factors among adult learners have significant bearing on their participation in adult education programmes. The conclusions drawn relating to such personality factors specifically are as follows:

- Majority of the subject belonging to active participants group have scored high on *Factor F*. This indicates that by and large the cheerful, active, impulsive. characteristics symbolic of high score of Factor F seems to promote the active participation of the subjects in adult education programmes;
- Majority of subjects belonging to drop-out group have scored high on *Factor I*. This shows that subjects having impatient and impractical outlook (characteristics of high scorers of Factors I may have a tendency to drop-out from adult education programmes;
- More than three fourth of subjects belonging to drop-out group have scored high on *Factor L*. This means the characteristics of high scoring subjects on this factor namely, mistrusting and doubtfulness seems to have a say on the phenomenon of drop-out;
- About 85% of the subjects belonging to active participants group have scored low on *Factor O*. This means that the matured, unanxious confidence possessed by the subjects (characteristics of low score on the factor) might influence positively the participation of subjects in adult education programmes.
- Good majority of subjects belonging to active participants group have scored low on *Factor Q2*. This shows that the needs namely, social approval and admiration (characteristics of low score on the factor) have some positive influence on the participation of subjects in adult education programmes.

Umayaparvathy (1982) based on her investigation about the impact of intelligence and achievement motivation on women attending literacy centers reported existence of significant difference in the level of attainment of literacy between the subjects representing high and low intelligence groups. Brist (1983) indicated that lack of flexibility and shyness on the part of adult learners were the factors leading to dropout. Seth *et.al.,* (1983) observed that learners who felt that they belonged to the group and were liked by others continued their participation in adult education programme.

Bishit (1983) reported that lack of flexibility on the part of adult learners and shyness exhibited by them were the factors responsible for poor achievement of learners attending adult education centers. Jayagopal (1985) through his case studies on learners observed that frustration, dejection, shyness, and conservatism as some of the factors that lead to the poor performance of learners from adult education centres.

Manjula (1986) identified some of the factors which affect adult learning and performance. The following are some of the factors which affect adult learning and performance:

(1) *Factors relating to adult learner*: There are certain factors within the adult learner which affect the process of adult learning:

(*a*) *Motivation*: Motivation may be assumed to be age-related. Positive motivation is always most welcome for adults. If adult learners have negative motivation, they certainly dislike and oppose;

(*b*) *Intelligence*: Apart from the variations in intelligence, the increase, decrease or stability in intelligence depends much on the psychometric devices used, and age of the learner;

(*c*) *Knowledge level:* If the learner does not know the code he can't understand the message. If he does not know anything about the subject-matter, he probably cannot understand it either. If he does not understand the nature of learning process itself, the chances are good that he will misperceive content, make incorrect inferences about the purposes or intentions of the instructor;

(*d*) *Ability to memorise*: Few adults may be good at long-term memory and some at short-term memory. The ability to retain information tends to be relatively stable among adults, if the material is short and meaningful. But on the whole they do not like to memorise things;

(*e*) *Home and family environment*: The environment in which an adult emerges, constitutes the major factors associated with adult learning. These are:

(*i*) General acceptance and encouragement from family to attend adult education centre;

(*ii*) availability of learning resources for adults at home; and

(*iii*) awareness of opportunities for organized learning for adults.

(*f*) *Personal disregard*: After the day's work they are not left with any energy to think, act or even react to their deplorable conditions. Lack of self-confidence, docility, submissiveness and vulnerability to exploitation are other factors which hamper the learning;

(*g*) *Social and environmental factors*: Impoverished conditions affect the learning ability and opportunities of the learners. Social values, role expectations and interests are other factors that facilitate and influence learning;

(*h*) *Communication skills:* If the learner does not have the ability to listen, to read to think, he will not be able to receive and decode the messages that the instructor has transmitted;

(*i*) *Attitude towards instructor and content*: The attitudes of a learner affect many ways in which he receives the message. The negative attitude toward the instructor affects the reception and understanding the message. Similarly if he does not believe in the value of the subject matter, it is difficult for him to understand clearly about it. Hence, adult learning is partly determined by his attitudes towards the instructor and the content of the message;

(*j*) *Attention toward the instruction*: Attention facilitates the most purposeful learning. The success of learning depends upon the attention of the learner toward the instructor;

(*k*) *Closed-mind*: Limited intellectual background, limited reading and narrow interests cause a person's mind to be narrow. This limits his understanding of human nature and makes him incapable of receiving messages fully;

(*l*) *Non-cognitive psycho-social factors*: These comprise memory, practice, approach and expectation.

Information processing and memory: Age-related individual differences in some aspects of information processing entailed in adult learning are:

(*a*) Attention to information (perception, meaning, persistence, association);

(*b*) Short-term and long-term memory-consists of input, stimulus-response, register, storage and retrieval (retention and recalling);

(*c*) Practice and reinforcement (rehearsal, record, conditioning);

(*d*) Pacing-Adults learn more effectively when they set their own pace of learning.

Approach: Adult learning is affected by the approach the adult takes to learning activity, which reflects: (*a*) previous experience; (*b*) use of learning procedure; and (*c*) current circumstances that give rise to the need for increased competence.

The previous experience of low achievement, and failures may reduce learning skills, persistence, self-confidence and participation in educational activities. Use of learning procedure results in increased knowledge and content competence. Current circumstances and recent role changes that call for adaptation, urging by significant others to obtain knowledge, help increased awareness of needs for competence, motivation and persistence:

(I) *Expectation*: Most adults approach learning with specific expectations about what they will gain from the experience, use of increased competence to achieve an external goal, interest in the subject contents, and enjoyment of the activity.

(II) *Factor relating to the instructor*: The following are some of the factors relating to the instructor which affect adult learning and performance:

(a) Ineffective environment: The environment created by the instructor affects the learning. The physical facilities, respect for other's point of view, recognition of accomplishments of others, permissiveness and rapport in general, are all important factors which affect the learning;

(b) Disorganized efforts: Disorganized efforts of the instructor affect the learning process;

(c) Standard of correctness: This involves the use of correct words or other symbols, and correct content or facts. Incorrect words, symbols, content and facts hamper the learning process;

(d) Poor communication skills: Lack of skill in writing and speaking obviously prevents the instruction from the instructor across to his learners. Poor reading habits and faulty listening are both psychological short-comings and are difficult to catch and correct;

(e) Inaccurate symbols: The system of symbols used to represent ideas, objects or concepts must be accurate and used skillfully. The crucial point in the usage of symbols to convey ideas is to select those that accurately represent the idea to be conveyed and is understood by the learners. Symbols are meaningful to a person only when he understands what they stand for;

(f) Attitudes: Instructors attitude affect instruction in at least three ways.

- *Attitudes towards self*: His attitude towards himself, are important. He should have the right attitude towards himself for effective teaching.
- *Attitude towards subject-matter*: The second factor is the attitude towards his subject-matter. His attitude quite often comes through in his messages. If he does not believe in the value of his subject-matter, it is difficult for him to communicate effectively about it.
- *Attitude towards learner*: The third kind of attitude that affects the instructors teaching behaviour is attitude towards his learner. The negative attitude toward the learners affects the instructor's message, and affects how people will respond to his instruction.

Proper understanding of the several characteristics of adults as learners is essential for helping adults to plan and organize their learning through self-direction and guidance. Alan Rogers (1986) provides a list of adult learner characteristics. He contends that adult learners consist of a wide variety of people, all having their own uniqueness:

- Some are more adults than others; while some opt to remain dependent, others search for autonomy;

- All are growing and developing; but in different directions and at different pace;
- Some hold a good deal of experience and knowledge, others bring less; and there are varying degrees of willingness and intention to use this resource for helping their learning process;
- They have a wide range of intentions and needs, some specific, some general, and related to subject matter; and some unknown even to themselves.

Kumaraswamy, (1992) conducted a study of certain factors related to achievement of adult learners. The variables considered were gender, age, caste general ability, achievement motivation, attitude and personality factors as measured by Cattell's 16 PF. With respect to personality factors on achievement the results of the study revealed the following:

- Possession of some of the personality traits like readiness to co-operate, adaptability, quickness in grasping ideas, cheerfulness, frankness, alertness, expression ability, worldliness, shrewdness, analytical ability, interest in intellectual matters and fundamental issues, and the like (represented by factors A, B, F, N, and Q1) by adult learners promoted better achievement in literacy skills i.e., reading, writing, numeracy and total achievement;
- The trend of the results (based on mean scores) indicated that possession of personality traits like rigidity, dull and sluggishness, evasive nature, depressiveness, fickle mindedness, withdrawing nature, shyness, lack of stability and will control by the learners may hamper the academic achievement of adult learners;
- Regression analysis considering adult learners achievement in literacy skills indicated that variables namely, attitude, general ability, achievement motivation, environmental stimulation and factor A

had significant impact on the achievement of adult learners.

Rajnani R. Shirur. (1997) identified the following assumptions made by Malcolm Knowles, relating to adult learning, which reflect some of the salient features of adulthood and are of primary concern to adult education:

- As a person matures, his/her self-concept moves from a dependent personality towards a self-directing human being;
- An adult accumulates a growing reservoir of experiences which serves as a rich learning resource. For an adult, personal experiences establish his self-identity and are considered highly valuable;
- The readiness of an adult to learn is closely related to the developmental tasks of his/her social roles; and
- There is a change in time perspective as individual matures, from one of future application of knowledge to immediacy of application.

Knowles (1980) has identified three main characteristics which sharply focus on the facilitators and barriers for new learning:

(*a*) Adults have more to contribute to the learning of others; for most kinds of learning, they are themselves a rich resource;

(*b*) Adults have a rich foundation of experience to which they can relate new experiences; and

(*c*) Adults have acquired a large number of fixed habits and patterns of thought and therefore tend to be less open minded.

Though the first two emphasize the relative value of experiences of adults as learning resource, the third forewarns adult educators against the rigidities and lack of responsiveness and sensitivities of adults and the consequent need for evolving appropriate learning strategies and methods.

Hemanta Kumar Khandai (2003) identified the following characteristics of adult learners which influence their learning abilities. An adult learner is a person who can not read, write or calculate. That means he is unskilled in writing his language. But it does not mean that he is ignorant or stupid. The adult learner has broad experience of life and difficult and complicated tasks. The characteristics of learners are as follows:

- Adult learners are voluntary learners who will leave if learning is not relevant to their needs, desires and capabilities;
- Adult learners have varied experiences, abilities, interests, attitudes, prejudices, habits, values and different levels of emotional maturity by learning and working in different kinds of environment;
- Adult learners require more time to practice new skills. In addition to this fact, retention is increased if practice immediately follows the initial learning;
- There exist individual differences among adult learners in terms of rate and quality of learning;
- They have many responsibilities, *viz.* in work place, at home and in the society. Hence, they have limited time, energy and money;
- Adult learners may have limited perception, limited vocabulary, poor self-confidence, unquestioning, obedience, excessive fatalism, rigidity and dogmatism as traits of their personality;
- They prefer to associate in the learning process and prefer to learn by participation;
- Adults evaluate learning in terms of results and its utility to their life situations;

- Adults have their own strategies and patterns of learning which they have found helpful to learn most quickly and most effectively;
- Adults with the advancement of age, have difficulty in seeing and hearing.

To sum up, there are limited studies undertaken on the influence of personality factors in relation to achievement of adult learners (Hand and Puder 1978; Bishit, 1983; Khajapeer, 1978; Jayagopal, 1985; Kumaraswamy, 1992). The representative studies dealing with characteristics of adults or learners behaviour of adult or factors influencing adult learning are reviewed. Keeping in view their implications to adult learning and to strengthen the need to consider the importance of research on learner related psychological issues. (Lawton 1951; Swamy, 1980; Varalakshmi, 1980; Venkatesulu, 1980; Reddy, 1981; Umayaparvathy, 1982; Seth et.al., 1983; Hemath Kumar Khandai, 2003; Ramadevi, 1962; Khan, 1964; Dellefield, 1965; Singh, 1967; Jain, 1969; Singh, 1969; Lokanadha Reddy, 1981; Manjula; 1986; Rajnani R.Shirur, 1997; Knowles, 1980; Lowe, 1975; Alan Rogers, 1986). The limited review on the influence of personality factors on adults learners achievement in literacy skills clearly demonstrates the need for such studies.

Studies on Attitude

Attitudes are generally considered as learned responses. An attitude is an orientation or a disposition or a sort of readiness to react in a certain way (to persons, things, situations, etc) which an individual carries with him in a sort of latent form; and it may become manifest in an individuals behaviour only when an occasion arises (in which he has to react to objects, persons etc). When an individual has to express his attitudes he may react to them in a predetermined manner (depending upon how he learned to react in his past life) either favourably or unfavourably or in an indifferent manner. All these responses may also depend upon the strength of his attitude towards a thing-or what one may call an object of his attitude obviously, an individual carries with him an array of attitudes some of which may be favourable or unfavourable, strong or weak. Similarly, because all attitudes are learned, they may undergo changes with new information or experience which an individual may acquire or undergo. In the course of learning of various attitudes, an individual might have developed certain type of attitude towards adult education. Possessing positive attitude towards education is believed to promote academic achievement of learners. Attempts were made by some researchers to explore the role of attitude of learners towards adult education on their achievement. Some of the representative studies are as follows: Studies examining the relationship between the attitude of adult learners towards literacy and its impact on their academic achievement are few in number. Some investigators like Sen (1951), Subramanyam and Mani (1964) attempted to find out whether learners had positive or negative attitude towards adult education. But they did not make any attempt to correlate attitude of learners with their level of achievement. Kapoor and Roy (1971) found that positive opinions towards education correlated positively with the acquisition of literacy skills in all groups.

Dixit (1975) in his study on educational need patterns of adults in the urban, rural and tribal communities of Rajasthan found that more than half of the respondents in urban population expressed that vocational training was very much helpful to them for their jobs. One fourth of the rural population indicated that they had literacy classes in the village which they could attend only at night. The majority of them had a favourable attitude towards adult education and vocation training.

Venkataiah (1978) studied the impact of Farmers Functional Literacy Programme on the participants in Andhra Pradesh. It was found that attitude towards adult literacy has significantly influenced the literacy performance of Functional Literacy Programme participants.

Madana Mohana Reddy (1980) conducted a study on opinion of adult learners towards National Adult Education Programme. Adult learners expressed positive opinion with respect to objectives of the programme, arrangements for popularising the programmes, materials provided to the centres, instructional arrangements and post-literacy and continuing education aspects. Gender, age and occupation have significantly influenced the opinion of adult learners towards National Adult Education Programme.

An attempt was made by Haragopal and Ravindar (1980) to assess the perceptions and attitude of the key functionaries who man the top and intermediate levels of adult education under National Adult Education Programme. The investigators have enquired about the recruitment practices in the field and the problems of the functionaries. The opinions of the key level functionaries were also obtained on teaching materials, role of voluntary organizations and practical problems/difficulties encountered in the implementation of the programmes and the solutions offered by them. The functionaries possessed positive attitude towards the programme and majority of problems were related to administration and adult learners.

Janardhan Naidu's (1980) study concentrated on the measurement of the attitudinal scores of adult education instructors towards various aspects relating to the National Adult Education Programme. The study revealed that majority of the instructors possessed a positive attitude towards adult and continuing education programmes.

Munuswamy (1980) measured the attitudes of the adult education organizers towards National Adult Education Programme. It was found that a good majority of the organizers were possessing positive attitude towards many aspects of the programme.

Nath (1981) studied the opinion of NSS Adult Education Organisers towards National Adult Education Programme.

He found that majority of the NSS organisers agreed with the follow-up aspects viz., financial aspects objectives, implementation agencies, instructional agencies, training and coverage, duration of the literacy centres of the NAEP. Simultaneously the investigator studied the effect of sex, age and educational qualifications on attitudes of the organisers.

Dey (1981) studied various aspects relating to the Adult Education Programme in Patamada Block in Bihar State. The investigator's main objective was to evaluate the programme and to know the basic characteristics of the instructors and their attitude towards the various aspects pertaining their main profession. More than 93 per cent of the instructors had no previous teaching experience. The instructors expressed favourable attitude with different physical facilities such as books, pencils, slates, lighting, blackboard and teaching charts available in the centres. The instructors expressed positive opinion with regard to the help received from their supervisors. Further, the study showed that majority of the instructors had a positive attitude towards adult and continuing education programmes, the facilities available with the center and the co-operation of the community in relation to the improvement of adult education centres.

Madras Institute of Developmental Studies (1982) revealed that more than 60 per cent of the learners had felt that the facilities provided at the centres were inadequate or unsatisfactory. The major complaints were that of inadequate space and lighting.

Susheela Mariappan (1982) conducted a study on "Learner's opinion in adult education centres of Tamil Nadu and Pondicherry". It was found that majority of men and women learners expressed positive opinion and their desire for literacy. However, a general observation was that the learners above 30 years were not keen to learn and were less interested in being educated. Men being more mobile and involved in social and civic affairs were found to be more knowledgeable.

Seth (1982), in this study on motivation of adult learners participating in the functional literacy Programme in Delhi, found that the educators were instrumental in sustaining the motivation of the participants in the Programme and this had influenced their attitude and the success of the Programme.

Lakshminarayana (1983) studied Adult Education among Tribals of Visakhapatnam District of Andhra Pradesh. The findings of the study are as follows: The maximum number of adult participants (94.96 per cent) was found to be below the age of 35 years. Majority of the participants (77.45 per cent) were found to be in the income range of Rs. 500-1500 a year. About 76.13 per cent of the participants stated that, because of heavy work, they could not attend the classes regularly and 50.40 per cent gave health problems as the reason. About 63.66 per cent said that they wanted to learn more about agriculture and 52.52 per cent about health. As many as 82.49 per cent expressed dissatisfaction of reading and writing materials in the centres.

Mohan (1983) conducted a study on 'Opinion of the instructors about the get up and contents of health and sanitation reader used in National Adult Education Programme'. The subjects of the study were instructors working in adult education centres. The sample of the study consisted of 106 instructors. The instructors had minimum education upto IX Class and some of them were educated upto degree level. The findings of the study revealed that: (1) Majority of the instructors felt that the size of the letters used in the primer was quite satisfactory. But there were a sufficient number of instructors who suggested the use of bold size letters than the one used in the primer; (2) Most of the instructors were satisfied with the paper and colour used for printing the primer; (3) Majority of the instructors were satisfied about the content areas and method of presenting the lessons.

Vasudeva Reddy (1983) enquired into the opinions of the National Adult Education Programme instructors relating to the usefulness of contents of reader intended to the learners. Majority of the instructors expressed favourable attitudes towards the programme and the materials.

Vijayalakshmi (1985) conducted a study on the attitude of adult education instructors towards their profession, benefits of adult education and current issues in adult education. The total samples of instructors were 130. Of which 100 were men and 30 were women. It was found that the instructors possessed a favourable attitude towards the profession which helped to organize the centres properly. Majority of the instructors expressed that they can attract the learners by promoting activities along with instruction, using local language as it will make the teaching / learning situation easier than by teaching in text book language.

Surya Mani and Reddy (1985) conducted a study on "Attitude and Job satisfaction of organizers working under Adult Education Programme". The findings of the study revealed that 72.22 per cent of the organizers belonged to moderately favorable attitude category and only 4.44 per cent of organizers had less favorable attitude towards adult education programmes.

Anuradha (1988) conducted a study on "Developing Positive Attitude amongst Adult Education Functionaries". It was found that the job conditions in this field were not attractive. Job was extremely tedious, time consuming and frustrating. It involved great deal of travelling which was difficult during nights in rural areas. The honorarium was very little, the morale of the workers was very low and attitudes and motivation were poor. It was suggested that steps should be taken to improve the field situation, training programmes should be well organized and that honorarium should be increased.

Arun Mishra and Kosthyal (1988) assessed the attitude of instructors towards adult education working under adult education unit of Garwal University. The objectives of the study were: (*i*) to find out attitudinal changes in the instructors due to training in adult education; (*ii*) to find difference in the attitudes of male and female instructors towards adult education; and (*iii*) to find out changes in their attitude during their active involvement in the programme. The results of the study indicated that significant difference existed between male and female instructors about their attitudes towards adult education. The female instructors showed more positive attitude than their male counterparts. The study showed that there existed sharp difference in pre and post-training attitude scores of the instructors towards adult education.

Kumaraswamy (1992) conducted a study ascertain factors related to achievement of adult learners. The sample of the study consisted of 240 neo-literates. Attitude towards adult education was on of the variables aimed to study its influence on the achievement of neo-literates. It was found that attitude has significantly influenced the performance of adult learners in reading, writing, numeracy and total achievement. The learners who obtained high scores on attitude also a high score on the sub-units of literacy and *vice versa*.

Sardar Patel Institute of Economics and Social Research, Ahmedabad (1993) evaluated the literacy campaign, Ahmedabad (Rural Gujarat). The agency observed that planning, implementation and monitoring of the literacy campaign was reasonably well designed despite numerous administrative, organisational, financial and socio-psychological constraints in the rural areas as perceived by learners. The agency viewed that adult education cannot be viewed in isolation. It is a part of overall development process and, therefore, its linkage with the other aspects of the growth need to be made more effective and durable.

Ramabrahmam *et al*. (1997) evaluated the total literacy campaign in East Godavari District. With regard to public opinion on environment building, it was found that artists were not satisfied with the way the cultural programmes were organized in tribal areas. They suffered due to lack of proper transport facilities. They expressed that their services were not optimally utilized during the campaign period.

Mastan (2000) conducted a study on the influence of training, attitude and community support on the performance of preraks organizing continuing education centers. It was found that gender, age, caste, education, marital status, income and experience significantly influenced the attitude of preraks. Better mean attitude scores were obtained by preraks representing women, 25-30 years age group, forward caste, intermediate qualified, married, higher income group and those possessing higher experience as preraks. It was also found that attitude significantly influenced the performance of preraks. High mean performance scores were obtained by the group having better attitude scores.

Thompson (2001) carried out a project on 'Transforming the Adult Education Agenda through the Kenya Post-literacy Project'. There are four interrelated objectives of the project, the first of which seeks to support policy and institutional reforms. To this end, a structural analysis study of the Board of Adult Education (BAE) and the Department of Adult Education (DAE) was conducted in 1996 prior to the commencement of implementation in the fifteen operational districts. The main objective of the study was to identify and analyze the core functions and structural constraints of both BAE and DAE, with a view to enhancing their efficiency and effectiveness. One of the justifications of the study was that it had been observed that there were overlaps in the functions of the BAE and DAE, resulting in duplication of work and dissipation of scarce financial and human resources. The lessons learnt through the project are as follows: There are value-added benefits which emerge from the adoption of an integrated approach to meeting the learning needs of adults and out-of-school youth. Recognition of system dynamics and the creative use of cultural, strategic, technical and political systems are critical pre-requisites for sound project management. It has been established that recognition and utilization of the wealth of the learners' previous knowledge and experience, perceptions and expectations facilitate learning, and enhance learner-centeredness and process-oriented project management. They also catalyze reflection on learning. An integrated development approach that is inclusive of the social, economic, cultural and political needs of the adult learners ensures effective management of change processes. Resistance to change at both the individual and organizational levels is common and should be expected. However, if it is not addressed creatively it has potential to stifle innovation. Consultation and democratization of the project implementation process facilitate faster and more acceptable achievement of project results.

Naresh Sharma (2001) conducted a study on Opinion of adult beneficiaries towards total literacy campaign in Dungarpur district of Rajasthan. The villages in Dungarpur district within the radius of 2-20 kms from the headquarters of Panchayat Samiti were arranged in three categories of 'high', 'medium' and 'low' population villages. Two villages from each the three cluster of villages were selected randomly 10 male and 10 female beneficiaries from each of the selected villages, in all 120 respondents (60 male and 60 female), in the age group of 15-35 years were chosen at random. It was concluded that majority of male and female beneficiaries had positive opinion towards total literacy campaign and there was no significant difference between the attitudes of male and female beneficiaries towards the total literacy campaign.

Reddeppa (2001) conducted a study on Jana Chaitanya Kendras in Chittoor District with special references to monitor effectiveness. It was found that the performance of monitors relating to different functions was influenced by their attitude towards adult education. With regard to functions, monitors with high positive attitude performed better with regard to literacy and post-literacy classes, charcha mandal activities, short term training programmes, sports and adventurous activities, cultural and entertainment programmes effectively.

Monitors with low positive attitude performed the role of maintaining the library and reading room effectively.

Vasudeva Rao, Viswanadha Gupta and Srinivasa Rao (2005) conducted a study on "Akshara Bharathi Programme: Volunteers' Perceptions" The investigator found that the problems of the volunteers were lack of honorarium and incentives, non availability of proper building to organize classes, delay in supply of primers / books in some centres, inconvenient location of the centres to learners, lack of awareness and understanding about the importance of education and objective of Akshara Bharathi programme among the masses.

Kulasekhar (2005) conducted a study on certain aspects of continuing education programme in Chittoor district, Andhra Pradesh with special reference to tribals. The sample of the study consisted of 280 neo-literates. The influence of attitude on the achievement of adult learners in reading, writing, numeracy and total achievement was found to be statistically significant. The mean scores obtained by low, medium and high scoring groups of attitude on: (*a*) reading test 22.88, 25.52, 30.98; (*b*) writing test are 16.67, 18.33, 20.77; (*c*) numeracy test are 16.65, 17.42, 21.60; and (*d*) total achievement are 56.63, 61.27 and 73.35. Hence, it can be stated that attitude of adult learners influences their achievement.

To sum up the studies conducted by Sen, 1951, Subramanyam and Mani, 1964; Kapoor and Roy, 1981; Venkataiah, 1978, Khajapeer, 1978; Kumaraswamy, 1992; Kulasekhar, 2005 have found that attitude towards adult education significantly influence the performance of adult learners in literacy skills with the inference that the higher the attitudes, the better will be the performance. Researchers like Dixit, 1975), Madana Mohan Reddy, (1980); Haragopal and Ravindar, (1980); Janardhan Naidu, (1980); Munaswamy, (1980), Nath, (1981); Dey, (1981); Madras Institute of Developmental Studies, (1982); Susheela Marriappan, (1982); Lakshminarayana, (1983), Seth, (1982); Vasudeva

Reddy,(1983), Vijayalakshmi,(1985); Surya Mani and Reddy,(1985); Anuradha, (1988); Arun Mishra and Kosthyal, (1988); Sardar Patel Institute of Economics and Social Research, Ahmedabad (1993); Mohan (1993), Rambrahmam *et al.* (1997); Mastan, (2000); Naresh Sharma, (2001); Reddeppa, (2001); Vasudeva Rao, Viswanadha Gupta and Srinivasa Rao (2005), Mohan, (1983) have attempted to know the opinions/ perceptions/attitudes of the functionaries like instructors, volunteers, preraks, supervisors, mandal literacy organizers, community members elite groups, mahila mandal on different aspects of the Total Literacy Campaign/Post Literacy/ Continuing Education programme (benefits of the programme, policy matters, teaching/learning materials, problems, job satisfaction training, administration etc). In view of the limited number of studies on the influence of attitude on the performance of neo-literates there is a need for further studies.

For the above review and sum up, it is clear that not many studies were undertaken by researchers on the performance of neo-literates in relation to personal, social, economic and psychological factors like personality factors and attitude. Hence the need for the present investigation.

3

Statement of the Problem

This chapter consists of statement of the problem, need for the study, scope of the study, objectives, hypotheses, variables studied, limitations and definition of the certain terms used in the study.

Statement of the Problem

"A Study on the Performance of Neo-literates in Relation to Certain Socio-Psychological Factors in Chittoor District".

Need for the Study

The socio-economic development of any country depends upon its educated citizens. India cannot achieve economic development, social transformation and effective social security until and unless the citizens are educated to the extent that enables them to participate in the country's developmental programmes, willingly, intelligently and effectively. Illiteracy as a mass phenomenon blocks economic and social progress, affects health and community hygiene, population control, national integration and security. Illiterate people tend to resist change and cling to traditionalistic forms of life. New ideas and new practices cannot be effectively communicated to those who are untrained to receive them and make use of them. Therefore, there is a need to reshape and change the attitude of masses through education and training. Adult Education emphasizes upon three main components namely, literacy, functionality and awareness. Literacy which is supposed to be a stepping stone for education includes the three rudimentary skills of reading, writing and numeracy and is considered as a minimum need for every human being to have a better life in the society. Functional literacy implies self-reliance in literacy and numeracy, becoming aware of the causes for their deprivation and moving towards amelioration of their conditions through organization and participation in the process of development, acquiring skills to improve the economic status and general well-being, imbibing the values of national integration, conservation of the environment, women's equality, observance of small family norms, etc. Functionality more or less is concerned with making the individual to function well individually, socially, culturally and economically. Adult education in India does not end with providing literacy, functionality and awareness. It extends further leading to life long education and continuing education. The scope of adult education extends to all sections of the community and it is a pre-condition to accelerate the pace and magnitude of development.

Recognising the need for the education of masses, India has implemented several literacy programmes especially after independence (Social Education Programme, 1949; Community Development Programme, 1951; Farmers' Functional Literacy Programme, 1966-67; Non-formal Education Programme, 1975; National Adult Education Programme, 1978; Point No.16 of the New 20 Point Programme, 1982; Mass Programme for Functional Literacy, 1986; National Literacy Mission, 1988) and Total Literacy Campaigns, 1989-90 onwards. The scheme of continuing education was introduced from 1995 onwards through the establishment of continuing education centres. Neo–literates are the main beneficiaries of continuing education Programme. The literacy rate of the country has increased from 16.67 in 1951 to 65.38 during 2001. As part of the National Literacy Mission, the Government of Andhra Pradesh has implemented total literacy campaigns, post-literacy and continuing education programmes, Akshara Sankranthi (2001-04), and Akshara Bharati Programmes (2 phases) (2005-06 and 2006-07). A good number of neo-literates are participating in the continuing education centres and it is necessary to know the level of proficiency they have achieved in literacy skills, and its associated factors.

Attainment in literacy skills refers to proficiency in 3 R's or reading, writing and numeracy skills. The total score obtained by the learner on all the three components of literacy can be stated as total achievement. How an individual has achieved proficiency in basic literacy skills depends upon how effectively he learns. Existing research studies in the field of adult education indicate that several socio-psychological factors and environmental factors operate and influence the learning behaviour, which ultimately decide the level of achievement of literacy skills by an individual.

Some research studies indicate that women achieve better than men and certain other studies indicate that men are better than women. Yet there are studies which denote that gender has no impact on the achievement. On the whole, there appears the need to explore the impact of gender on the achievement of neo-literates who are attending the continuing education centres. Age is yet another important variable which deserves attention. Some research studies (vide chapter II) have shown that the lower age group have performed better in achieving literacy skills whereas some others have found that high age group have performed better in literacy skills. Further, there are studies which have revealed that age has no impact on the achievement of neo-literates. Hence there is need to explore the impact of age on the performance of neo-literates attending the continuing education centres. With age comes growth and with growth, an individual's fund of experience involving a wide variety of situations increases steadily. Experience helps an individual to modify his behaviour and method of dealing with situations so that he may become more efficient. Hence, age in as much as it reflects the degree of maturity and experience may affect the achievement of an individual.

In India people representing Scheduled Castes and Scheduled Tribes are deprived of certain economic and social benefits as a result of which some of these people may lack confidence regarding their own abilities and capacities. This may lead to variation in the achievement between learners representing Scheduled Castes and Scheduled Tribes *versus* other castes. Hence, there appears the need to know the impact of caste on achievement of learners. In a similar manner there is need to know the influence of income and marital status on the performance of neo-literates.

In addition to the above, personality is another variable that has potential influence on learners achievement in literacy skills. Personality characteristics like introversion, extroversion, emotional maturity, flexibility, anxiety, imaginativeness, boldness, conservatism, fatalism, cheerfulness, and the like influence the behaviour of a person in carrying out a task. It is likely that neo-literates with different levels of their personality characteristics may differ in the manner in which they go about in achieving literacy skills. Therefore, it would be of interest to examine how personality factors are related to the achievement of the neo-literates.

Attitude has a major role to play in enabling the learners to participate in the literacy centres. In operational terms, attitude refers to the details of what people think or feel on the way in which they intend to act. It may be generally around that attitude of a learner towards various aspects of adult education Programme like benefits, community support, instruction, supervision, enhance his level of achievement. Some of the studies as presented in chapter II have revealed that attitude influences the performance of adult learners/ neo-literates and the studies are quite limited. Hence there is need for empirical investigations relating to the impact of attitude on the performance of neo-literates.

In the light of the forgoing considerations, it may be assumed that differences in personal factors (gender, age), social factors (caste, marital status), economic factors (occupation, income), and personality factors (16 PF and attitude) may significantly influence the performance of neo-literates attending the continuing education centres.

Scope of the Study

The Government of India and non-government organisations are making a lot of efforts to eradicate illiteracy in our country. The effective implementation of total literacy campaigns has contributed towards the substantial increase of neo-literates and semi-literates. But due to lack of immediate post-literacy activities at the grassroot level and due to lack of people's participation in the continuing education centres the neo-literates and semi-literates are again relapsing into illiteracy. The non-enrolment and dropout at primary level and at adult education centres, poor socio-economic conditions are other reasons is leading to the problem of illiteracy in the country. How to check the problem? What types of efforts are basically required to promote adult education in the country and at the global level. Studies that deal with the basic aspects of learning or achievement in relation to different personal, social, economic and programme related factors would be of immense help to the programme planners and executives to design effective strategies. The present study which is related to the on-going programme of adult education would be of greater help to the district administrations and National Literacy Mission to chalk out effective strategies for promoting the literacy, post-literacy and continuing education programmes.

Objectives of the Study

1. To study the influence of personal, social and economic factors (gender, age, caste, marital status, occupation and income) on the achievement of neo-literates;
2. To know the influence of personality factors (as measured by Cattell's 16 PF) on the achievement of neo-literates;
3. To estimate the impact of attitude of neo-literates on their achievement;
4. To understand the contribution of different independent variables to achievement of neo-literates in literacy skills.

Hypotheses

Based on the above objective, the following hypotheses were formulated for testing. Each variable was tested separately:

1. Gender does not significantly influence the achievement of neo-literates in literacy skills and total achievement;
2. Age does not significantly influence the achievement of neo-literates in literacy skills and total achievement;
3. Caste does not significantly influence the achievement of neo-literates in literacy skills and total achievement;
4. Occupation does not significantly influence the achievement of neo-literates in literacy skills and total achievement;
5. Marital status does not significantly influence the achievement of neo-literates in literacy skills and total achievement;
6. Income does not significantly influence the achievement of neo-literates in literacy skills and total achievement;

7. Personality factors (as measured by Cattell's 16 PF) do not significantly influence the achievement of neo-literates in literacy skills and total achievement;
8. Attitude does not significantly influence the achievement neo-literates in literacy skills and total achievement;
9. No single variable or a set of variables included in the study do not significantly exert their contribution to the reading achievement of neo-literates;
10. No single variable or a set of variables included in the study do not significantly exert their contribution to the writing achievement of neo-literates;
11. No single variable or a set of variables included in the study do not significantly exert their contribution to the numeracy achievement of neo-literates;
12. No single variable or a set of variables included in the study do not significantly exert their contribution to the total achievement of neo-literates.

Variables Studied

Dependent Variables

Achievement of neo-literates in literacy skills: 1. Reading; 2. Writing; 3. Numeracy; and 4. Total achievement which is the total score on reading, writing and numeracy.

Independent Variables

The independent variables included in the study are:

1.	Gender	(Male, Female)
2.	Age	(15-25 years, 25-35 years, 35 years and above)
3.	Caste	(Forward, Backward, Scheduled Castes and Scheduled Tribes)
4.	Occupation	(Agriculture, Non-agriculture)

5.	Marital Status	(Married and Unmarried)
6.	Income	(Below Rs. 10,000 per year and Rs. 10,000 and above per year)
7.	Personality factors	Cattell's 16 PF
8.	Attitude	Towards Programme inputs (environment building, physical facilities, materials, Community support, instruction, monitoring, supervision, post-literacy activities).

Limitations

1. The study is limited to Chittoor district
2. The study is limited to neo-literates attending continuing education centres. The study does not consider under which programme the sample were made literate. It is due to lack availability of various registers of the programmes.
3. The study is limited to a few personal, social, economic and personality factors (16 PF and attitude).

Definition of Certain Terms

Neo-literate

A neo-literate is a person who has just completed his course in adult education centre and provided with a neo-literate certificate by the Zilla Sakharatha Samithi, Chittoor, which happens to be the agency for implementing adult and continuing education programmes. In the context of the study neo-literate or adult learner are used inter-changeably.

Prerak

A motivator and organizer of continuing education centre. He has to organize the literacy centres, reading room, library, charcha mandal, simple and short duration training programmes and keep the continuing education centre as a window for receiving information and as a centre for communication and development activities.

In the context of Chittoor district, preraks are kept responsible for covering illiterates, semi-literates and to organize continuing education centres for neo-literates and others. A Prerak has to serve as a literacy volunteer for Akshara Sankranthi and Akshara Bharati Programmes as per the directions of Zilla Saksharatha Samiti, Chittoor.

Performance/Achievement

In the context of the study, performance or achievement are interchangeably used which refer to the performance of the neo-literates in literacy skills i.e., reading, writing and numeracy skills.

Monitor

A person who has been organizing post literacy centre after literacy campaign in Chittoor District.

Functional Literacy

As specified in the National Literacy Mission document (1988) by Government of India, functional literacy implies achieving self-reliance in literacy and numeracy by learners, becoming aware of the causes of their deprivation and moving towards amelioration of their conditions through organization and participation in the process of development, acquiring skills to improve the economic status and general well-being, imbibing the values of national integration, conservation of the environment, women's equality, observance of small family norms etc.

Adult Learners

The term 'adult learners' used in the context of the present study refers to the neo-literates who are attending the continuing education centres.

Equivalency Programmes

These are one type of continuing education programmes which provide an opportunity to adults and out of school children who have acquired basic literacy skills or who have completed primary education and who are willing to continue their education beyond elementary literacy for acquisition of competencies equivalent to primary or secondary levels of formal education. Equivalency programmes are, therefore, designed as alternative education programmes equal to existing formal, general or vocational education.

Income Generating Programmes

Income generating programmes are those vocational and technical programmes which help participants to acquire or upgrade vocational skills and enable them to conduct income generating activities. There can be a variety of income generating programmes delivered in a wide variety of contexts taking into account the local needs and interests of learners.

Quality of Life Improvement Programmes

These are especially significant type of educational programmes designed to enhance the well being of citizens. These aim to equip learners and community with knowledge, skills, attitude and values to enable them to improve quality of life as individuals and members of the community.

Individual Interest Promotion Programmes

These continuing education programmes aim to provide opportunity to individuals to participate in and learn about their social, cultural, spiritual, health, physical and artistic interests. The focus of individual interest promotion programmes is on personnel development by providing opportunities for promotion of specialized individual interests which may lead to improvement in the quality of human resources of the society.

Continuing Education

Continuing education is one of the hallmarks of a learning society. It is based on the premise that all adults should be entitled to continued opportunities for education throughout their lives. It recognises learning wherever it takes place—not only within the premises of organized institutions but also in the work place, home and other places. Even those who have had the most advanced education will be required to upgrade their knowledge. The broader concept of continuing education emphasizes the need of neo-literates for life long opportunities for education and training. Continuing education which provides a second chance to those who missed formal education is responsive to the needs of learners and directly addresses structural inequalities in society. It is now emerging as one of the most important components of education as a whole and it includes all learning opportunities outside the basic literacy and primary education. It is in fact a continuum of basic literacy and post-literacy phase and visualized as an attempt to provide systematic, organized and well co-ordinated mechanism to mobilise all the resources in support of literacy, post-literacy and continuing education in the perspective of life long education.

Post-literacy

The concept of post-literacy refers to those efforts carried out after literacy phase, the objectives of which are remedial (taking care of those persons who have not achieved adequate levels of literacy), continuation (with would enable the neo-literates transform from a guided learning situation to a self-learning situation, application of literacy skills to improve quality of life) and community participation (where community participation and action for social development is initiated).

Attitude Towards Adult Education

In the context of the study attitude relates to the attitude of neo-literates towards the benefits of literacy, physical facilities, materials, community support, prerak qualities, activities of preraks.

The method adopted in the study in terms of construction of research tools, sample chosen, data collection, statistical techniques employed are presented in Chapter-IV.

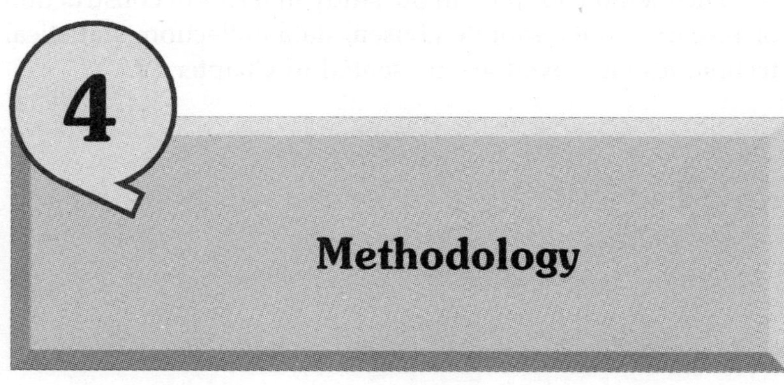

4 Methodology

The testing of the hypotheses framed in the previous chapter required the measures namely, achievement test for measuring reading, writing and numeracy skills of the neo-literates, measure of attitude of neo-literates and personality test. Personality characteristics were studied by using Cattell's 16 PF test (Form E) on literacy skills. Achievement and attitude of neo-literates towards adult education were measured through tools that were devised for the purpose of the study. Personal information sheet was used to know the gender, age, caste, occupation, marital status and income of the subjects.

Measure of Achievement

For the purpose of the present study, a test that can measure the achievement of neo-literates was necessary. Measuring achievement of neo-literates means, estimating the level of attainment in reading, writing and numeracy skills (3 R's). An adult who has successfully completed the course in an adult education centre should have achieved basic skills of reading, writing and arithmetic to the extent of fulfilling the norms of literacy and numeracy stipulated by Nationality Literacy Mission.

Keeping the norms in view, the functionaries in the field of adult education seemed to have developed achievement tests in their own way to measure the final outcome of adult education programme. Examination of some of the tests developed in various projects in Andhra Pradesh to test the achievement of neo-literates revealed that they were based more or less on common sense. This necessitated the investigator to plan and develop an achievement test suitable for testing the achievement of the sample of the present study. The following procedure was followed to develop the test.

1. To start with, the source of the test items and the nature of the test were thought of. The government of Andhra Pradesh has published three primers in regional language (Telugu) for use in adult education projects of the state. These were taken as the source material for testing the knowledge of neo-literates.
2. The comprehensive idea about the achievement of neo-literates can be possible only when the achievement is measured in all the three areas *viz.*, reading ability, writing ability and numeracy skill. Hence, an achievement test developed should include all these three areas.

Keeping the above in view, in order to develop a standard achievement test, a panel of experts from the field functionaries who can assist the investigator in the development of the test was thought of. An experts panel consisting of 3 university level teachers, 10 Mandal Literacy Organisers and 10 Preraks (with good educational background) was drawn randomly from the list of preraks and Mandal Literacy Organizers obtained from Zilla Saksharatha Samithi, Chittoor district i.e., area of the study. Each of the members of the expert panel thus drawn were interviewed for knowing their opinion about the way the achievement test should be. The following suggestions were provided by them:

1. There should be separate tests for each of the units (reading, writing and numeracy), as per National Literacy Mission norms;
2. The reading test should be for 40 marks, writing test for 30 marks and numeracy test for 30 marks. The total test should be for 100 marks. As per the National Literacy Mission norms, to declare a person as literate he/she has to obtain 50 per cent of marks in each of the three components and 70 per cent as an aggregate. This should be duly followed;
3. The item should be drawn from the primers and neo-literate materials used in the district. They should be locally relevant;
4. The items should as far as possible related to the primers and should be based on the psychological principles of known to unknown, and simple to difficult;
5. The investigator should prepare 3-4 items for each of the sub-units of the reading, writing and numeracy tests for drawing the suitable ones.
6. They should be presented to the panel of experts for checking the relevance, suitability and retention of items for the pilot study.
7. The possible items for sub-units of the test may be as follows. Reading test, (reading of letters, words, paragraph, sentences based on message, identification of figures, matching of the words, comprehension etc). Writing test (writing of words, writing of sentences, comprehension passage, identification of figures/symbols, writing of a letter etc).Numeracy test (writing the numbers, simple mathematical operations including two or three digits, simple statement sums involving addition, subtraction,

multiplication, division, items on time, weights and measures, distance, writing of date based on the calendar etc).

Keeping the above in view, the investigator pooled the items and prepared the preliminary forms of the test with 4 items for each. The panel were requested to go through the items and suggest modifications. Out of 4 items for each 2 were deleted and the remaining two were retained for the pilot study by the expert group. The preliminary form of items of the sub-test thus finalized were administered to a sample of 100 neo-literates in order retain one of the items based on difficulty and discrimination levels. The data thus obtained was analysed to find out the differences and discrimination level. As suggested by Garrot (1979) all the items showing discrimination values of 0.30, and above and difficulty values between 0.40 and 0.60, were considered for inclusion in the final form and the rest were ignored. The details of the test items are as follows:

I. Reading Test

Reading test is intended to identify the level of reading abilities and proficiency achieved by the participants of the programme. Items for the reading test were drawn from the primers and post-literacy materials used in the centres. The details of the reading test are as follows :

(a) ***Identification of words based on figures***: The figures and words for this purpose were drawn from the primers. Further, they were locally relevant. The subject has to identify the figures, read the words and put a tick mark to the appropriate ones.

(b) ***Matching of words:*** The subject has to match the relevant words with pencil after reading them.

(c) ***Comprehension passage:*** A single passage relating to self help groups was given. The passage has 26 words. The sample of neo-literates were supposed to read the passage loudly and answer 5 questions based on the passage. Two alterative answers are given for each question. The subject has to read them and put a tick mark to the correct one.

(d) **Identification of figures:** 5 figures relating to day life were given. The subject has to identify the figures.

The items of the final form of reading test and the scoring of the test is detailed fellow:

Scoring Procedure

Sl.No.	Item	Marks
I.	Identification words based on figures	5
II.	Matching of the words	5
III.	Comprehensive Passage (10+15)— For reading passage at poor level 3 marks, at average level 6 marks, at above average/good level 10 marks and for correctly answering each question 3 marks (3x5=15 marks)	25
IV.	Identification of figures	5
	Total	**40**

II. Writing Test

The details of the writing test are as follows:

(a) Writing the names of figures: 5 figures which were locally familiar were given. The subject has to identify the figures and write their names.

(b) Neo-literates background information: The subject has to write his / her name, father's name, village name, mandal name and name of the district.

(c) Fill in the blanks: 5 sentences which were drawn from the primers / neo-literate materials were given and the last word of the sentence was left blank in brackets in a shuffled manner and given at the top. The subject

has to read the sentences and words and has to write appropriate words in each sentence.

(d) ***Comprehension passage:*** A comprehension passage dealing with literacy and population of the country was given. The passage has 32 words. The samples of learners were supposed to read the passage and write the answers for the 5 questions relating to the passage.

The items of the final form of writing test and the scoring procedure of the test is detailed below:

Scoring Procedure

Sl.No.	Item	Marks
I.	Writing the names of figures	5
II.	Neo-literate's background information	5
III.	Fill in the blanks	5
IV.	Writing answers to comprehension passage	15
	Total	**30**

III. Numeracy Test

The details of numeracy test are as follows:

(a) ***Fill in the blanks with numbers:*** In a given sequence of a numbers there are blanks and the subject has to fill in the blanks with appropriate numbers.

(b) ***Addition:*** Three additions covering 2 or 3 digits are provided and the subject has to do the additions.

(c) ***Subtractions:*** Three subtractions involving 2 or 3 digits are provided and the subject has to do the subtractions.

(d) ***Divisions:*** Three divisions involving 2 or 3 digits with a simple number are provided and the subject has to do the divisions.

(e) **Statement sums:** Two statement sums one involving multiplication and the other involving division are provided and the subject has to do the sums.

(f) **Fill in the blanks:** 5 fill in the blanks dealing with weights, measures and time are provided and the subject has to fill up the blanks.

(g) **Depicted time:** Two items indicating the time in the watches are provided and the subject has to write the timings in the given watches.

Scoring Procedure

Sl.No.	Item	Marks
I.	Writing the missing numbers	5
II.	Simple additions (3), subtractions (3), multiplications (3) and divisions (3) (1 mark for each item)	12
III.	Statement sums 2 Numbers x 3 marks = 6 marks	6
IV.	Fill in the blanks	5
V.	Identification of time in the watches	2
	Total	**30**

A model test paper with double the number of items was submitted to panel of 5 subject experts for their comments they were requested to give suggestions for improvement and their suggestions were incorporated. Then the test was administered 100 neo-literates to know the discrination and difficulty levels. The data thus obtained were analysed to find out the difficulty and discrimination levels of each of the items included in the test paper. Items showing discrimination value of 0.30 and above and difficulty values between 0.40 and 0.60 were included in the final form. The final form of the literacy test is appended.

Validity and Reliability

The test developed for measuring a particular aspect will be considered appropriate only when its validity is true. The achievement test in 3 R's, developed on the lines described above, (based on review, primers, experts suggestions, pilot study) possessed satisfactory validity with reference to the content validity. The test rest method was followed for establishing reliability and the total test was administered to a sample of 100 learners with a gap of 3 weeks. The correlation co-efficients obtained were 0.72 (reading test), 0.69(writing test), 0.65 (numeracy test) which were significant as 0.01 level.

Measure of Personality

A measure of personality was used to know whether there was any relationship between personality characteristics and achievement of neo-literates. Cattell's 16 Personality factor questionnaire was used in the present study as it provides a fairly reliable, quick and at the same time a reasonably complete measure of personality characteristics. There are various forms of Cattell's 16 PF questionnaires *i.e.,* Form A, Form B, Form C and Form E. Among them, Forms A, B and C are intended for well educated individuals and Form E for low educated individuals. Since neo-literates who had attained basic literacy skills and represent low education level category, Form E of Cattell's 16 PF questionnaire was considered appropriate for the purpose of the present study.

The personality factors measured by form E and those covered in Forms A, B and C are one and the same. Further, form E is fairly a short inventory than other forms and has the advantage of ease of administration and scoring. In addition, the 16 PF (Form E) has several advantages over many single scale tests. They are as follows: (1) The total picture of personality using all the 16 personality factors is a better predictor than what may be obtained from the single scale tests; (2) The 16 personality factors are essentially independent factors and the correlations among them are usually negligible; (3) The vocabulary involved is elementary and can be easily understood; (4) The test has an index to guard against any motivational distortions that may be present. In view of the above listed advantages of the 16 PF questionnaire (Form E), it was adopted for use in the present investigation. As this form was originally in English, a translated version of it into the regional language (Telugu) was necessary as the respondents of the present study happen to be Telugu speaking people and had no knowledge of English.

The Telugu version of the form was already used by Reddy (1981) and found to give satisfactory results on similar type of subjects. However, this Telugu version was again subjected to scrutiny by 5 experts (university level teachers working in the departments of education and psychology) who were well versed in Telugu as well as the subject matter. Their suggestions were carried out wherever necessary. This was done in order to see that during translation, the meaning and function of each of the statements in the questionnaire was not disturbed in any way. Further, both the English and Telugu versions of the test were administered to 100 subjects having good proficiency both in Telugu and English with an interval of three weeks. The reliability indices for both versions were between 0.72 to 0.68. In addition, the Telugu version thus obtained was also subjected to test-retest reliability by administering it to 100 neo-literates with an interval of three weeks. Reliability for this (0.66) was fairly satisfactory to adopt and administer the test in the translated version and rely upon the scores obtained thereby. The procedure of administration and the scoring of the 16 PF questionnaire (Form E) was essentially the same as described in the manual (original English form). The questionnaire is appended.

Measure of Attitude

A measure that can rate attitude of neo-literates towards adult education was needed for the purpose of the present investigation. From the review of literature (vide Chapter 2) it is clear that there were no suitable standardized tests to measure the attitude of neo-literates towards adult education which includes (benefits, physical facilities, materials, community support, prerak qualities, activities of preraks/ others). In view of this, the investigator has to develop an attitude measure to suit the purpose of the present study.

Various methods were followed in attitude measurement like Thurstone method, Likert method, Semantic differential and so on. In the context of the present investigation, development of attitude measure based on Likert method of attitude scale construction was considered more appropriate. The Likert method was preferred over the other methods due to certain advantages namely: (*a*) the scale construction procedure was easier and simpler; (*b*) the technique was claimed to provide more information about subjects attitude since the responses would be given to each of the many items; and (*c*) the method was relatively more reliable, valid and better understood. In order to develop the scale, an experts panel consisting of 3 university level teachers, 10 mandal literacy organizers and 10 preraks with good educational background was drawn and they were the same group who assisted in the preparation and finalization of the achievement test.

For the preparation of the preliminary form first, the nature and scope of the statements that were to be included in the proposed attitude scale were examined in the light of the operational definition of the concept 'Attitude towards adult education'. All the favourable or unfavourable statements that were suggested to indicate the attitude of the neo-literates on various aspects of adult education were pooled together from the available literature. The statements were further supplemented by interviewing various field functionaries and community representatives chosen randomly from the district.

They were asked to list either favourable or unfavourable statements that were supposed to indicate attitude towards adult education programme aspects as mentioned earlier. The statements thus obtained were subjected to scrutiny and relevant ones were chosen and added to the list. After this, in order to avoid ambiguity and overlapping, all the statements together were reviewed and rewritten after consulting the panel of experts.

The preliminary form, thus prepared, consisted of 55 statements of which 28 were supposed to represent positive attitude and the remaining 27 statements negative attitude towards adult education. This was presented to the panel of experts with a request to suggest improvements wherever necessary. The suggestions of the experts were carried out. In all, 50 statements remained in preliminary form of which fifty per cent were supposed to represent negative attitude towards adult education and the rest positive attitude.

The preliminary form of the attitude measure thus formulated was administered to 50 neo-literates (chosen randomly) from the continuing education centres of the district in order to examine whether the statements were easily understood by the learners and to know whether they possessed clarity or not. In the light of experience gained improvements were carried out in the statements wherever necessary. Then, the positive and negative statements were mixed together with the help of random numbers. While doing this, the sequence of the statements was maintained as far as possible (the assistance of the university level teachers was taken here also). After this, the preliminary form of the attitude scale was subjected to standardisation.

Rating Procedure for the Statements

Before taking up standardization, the way the neo-literates of the sample have to rate each statement in the final form was also determined. In doing so, the background of the subjects of the sample and the opinion of the experts (who assisted in the scrutiny of the statements of the preliminary form) were kept in view. It was thought appropriate to consider the rating that would be as simple as possible in order to help the neo-literates to indicate their rating with ease. The numerical rating scale consisting of 5 descriptive cues, *viz.*, Strongly Agree, Agree, Undecided, Disagree and Strongly Disagree, was chosen considering it as appropriate one for the sample. The neo-literates were supposed to agree with any of the above alternative cues provided against each statement to indicate the intensity of their attitude towards adult education.

Procedure of Standardization

The purpose of the present attitude test was to measure the quantum of positive/negative attitude possessed by the neo-literates towards adult education programme aspects. In view of this, neo-literates who had just completed the course were considered as appropriate sample for standardization of the measure. Hence, a sample of 100 neo-literates was chosen randomly from different continuing education centres in the district. The measure was administered to each of the neo-literates of the sample individually by the investigator. The instructions relating to the method of indicating responses to the statements in the measure were first read out to the subjects.

Scoring of the Statement

For the purpose of scoring of the statements, numerical values were assigned to the five categories of responses (rating) against each statement. The following numerical values were assigned to the ratings of positive/negative statements in the scale.

Sl.No.	Nature of Response	Numerical Value Assigned	
		Positive Statement	Negative Statement
1.	Strongly Agree	5	1
2.	Agree	4	2
3.	Undecided	3	3
4.	Disagree	2	4
5.	Strongly Disagree	1	5

Selection of the Statements

The 't' test values for each of the statements of the measure were calculated to find out the discrimination power and usefulness of the statements chosen. Statements that had calculated 't' value equal to or greater than 1.96 were selected for inclusion in the final form. All the other statements with 't' value less than 1.96 were discarded. As per this procedure, 10 statements were discarded and 40 statements, having 20 positive and 20 negative statements remained in final form.

Reliability of the Measure

An attitude test developed to measure the attitude of specific group of individuals representing specific category will be sound on establishment of its reliability. In order to find the effectiveness of the attitude measure developed, its test-retest reliability was examined by obtaining ratings for the measure with an interval of two weeks between the first and second administration of the measure to the same set of 100 neo-literates. The correlation co-efficient between the ratings was 0.68 which was significant at 0.01 level. Hence, the measure may be considered as having high reliability.

Validity of the Scale

Validity is another criteria considered to estimate the appropriateness of any measure developed to examine a particular aspect of an individual's attitude. The attitude measure of the present study developed on the lines described above indicated satisfying content validity, item (statement) validity and intrinsic validity. The details relating to them are as described below:

Content Validity

Content validity refers to the establishment and evaluation of the significance of the test items individually and as a whole. Every item should be a sampling of that aspect which the test purports to measure. In addition, items should collectively constitute a representative sample of the variable that is measured.

As already described, items for the measure were collected from different sources *viz.*, review of literature, adult education project officers, mandal literacy organizers, preraks, neo-literates and community representatives. In addition, it was also supplemented by interviewing selected neo-literates and experts to make sure that all possible items were covered. Thus, it can be reasonably assumed that the attitude scale developed possesses satisfactory content validity.

Item Validity

Item validity stresses the number of discriminations of the desired sort that the item is capable of making. It stresses the extent to which the item predicts segregation of respondents into those with high versus low criterion scores. The discriminative power of each of the items of the present measure was established by calculating their 't' values. Thus, the items chosen for the measure were found to be satisfactorily valid.

Intrinsic Validity

According to Guilford (1954), intrinsic validity indicates the degree to which the test measures what it purports to measure. This in other words means verification of how well the obtained scores measure the test true score component. Intrinsic validity of a test is expressed in terms of square root its reliability value. Thus, the intrinsic validity of the attitude measure developed was 0.68=0.82 which can be assumed as highly satisfactory intrinsic validity. The final form of attitude scale is appended.

Selection of the Sample

Chittoor district happens to be one of the successful districts in implementing literacy campaigns. The district consists of 3 revenue divisions and 66 mandals. Continuing education centres are organized in all the revenue divisions and mandals. Preraks are given the responsibility of covering the non-literates, dropouts, newly attained age groups remaining illiterate through the centres. Multi-stage random sampling method was used for selecting the sample. At the first stage 6 mandals were randomly selected. Each mandal consists of 15-25 continuing education centres. At the second stage, 5 continuing education centres were randomly selected. From each of the continuing education centres at the third stage a sample of 12 neo-literates were randomly selected. Thus the sample of the study was 360 neo-literates (6 x 5 x 12 = 360 learners)

The lists of the centres and preraks organizing continuing education centres were collected from the office of the Zilla Saksharatha Samathi, Chittoor. The lists of neo-literates were collected from the prerak in order to select the neo-literates by adopting simple random sampling.

Collection of Data

The data required for the study was collected from the learners by contacting them individually at the centres. Necessary rapport was established before collecting the data from them. The help of the Prerak was sought by the investigator in administering the tools. The measures were administered to the learners in two sessions. In the first session, achievement test was administered. During the second session, measures of attitude, and 16 PF questionnaire were administered. An interval of 15-30 minutes was given between the administrations of the tests. It took approximately two hours for the completion of all the tools by each neo-literate. Personal data relating to the learner's name, gender, age, caste, occupation, marital status and income was collected by utilizing the personal data sheet. Thus the final data relating to study was collected.

Analysis of Data

The data collected was analysed by using relevant statistical techniques like 't' test and 'F' test to find out the differences among the groups. The multiple correlation 'R' was calculated by carrying out stepwise regression analysis.

In the next chapter, results and discussion are presented.

5 Results and Discussion

The objectives of the study are:

1. To study the influence of personal, social and economic factors (gender, age, caste, marital status, occupation and income) on the achievement of neo-literates;
2. To know the influence of personality factors (as measured by Cattell's 16 PF) on the achievement of neo-literates;
3. To estimate the impact of attitude of neo-literates on their achievement;
4. To understand the contribution of different independent variables to achievement of neo-literates in literacy skills.

Keeping the objectives in view, the results of the study are presented, in this chapter as follows:

I. Distribution of the sample as per variables;

II. Literacy achievement among the sample as per National Literacy Mission Norms;

III. Distribution of performance scores;
IV. Influence of personal variables on achievement (Gender and Age).
V. Influence of social variables on achievement (Caste and marital status)
VI. Influence of economic variables on achievement (Occupation and Income)
VI. Influence of personality factors on achievement (16 Factors)
VII. Influence of attitude on achievement
VIII. Correlation Matrices
IX. Multiple Regression Analysis

Distribution of the Sample as per Variables

In the present study an attempt has been made to know the distribution of respondents of various groups as per variables, the details of which are as presented in Table 5.1. It can be observed from the table that there are 55.00 per cent of women in the sample and the remaining 45.00 per cent belonged to men category.

In the present study 3 age groups were considered. 43.05 per cent of the sample belonged to 15-25 years, 25.00 per cent belonged to 25-35 years and the remaining 31.95 per cent belonged to 35 years and above age group.

Caste gives sanction for recognition and acceptance, in ones own community. Human being on his historically the Indian society is stratified in to a hierarchy of castes. Out of the total respondents 47.22 per cent belonged to forward castes 33.61 per cent belonged to backward castes and 19.67 per cent belonged to scheduled castes and scheduled tribes.

For the purpose of the present study two occupation groups were considered *i.e.,* agriculture and non-agriculture. Agriculture activities refer to possessing self land or working

Table 5.1 : Distribution of the Sample as per Variable

Sl. No.	Group	N	Percentage
I.	**Personal Variables**		
1.	*Gender*		
	(*a*) Male	162	45.00
	(*b*) Female	198	55.00
2.	*Age*		
	(*a*) 15 - 25 years	155	43.05
	(*b*) 25 - 35 years	90	25.00
	(*c*) 35 and above years	115	31.95
II.	**Social Variables**		
1.	*Caste*		
	(*a*) Forward	170	47.22
	(*b*) Backward	121	33.61
	(*c*) SCs & STs	69	19.17
2.	*Marital Status*		
	(*a*) Married	240	66.67
	(*b*) Unmarried	120	33.33
III.	**Economic Variables**		
1.	*Occupation*		
	(*a*) Agriculture	193	53.61
	(*b*) Non-agriculture	167	46.39
2.	*Income*		
	(*a*) Below Rs.10,000/- per year	196	54.44
	(*b*) Rs.10,000 and above per year	164	45.56

in the lands of others for remuneration or engaged in the activities like cutting, sowing, harvesting etc. Non-agriculture group refers to those engaged in tailoring, brick making, business activities, road laying, forest products collection etc.

About two–thirds of the sample are represented by married group and the remaining one-third of the sample are unmarried. The occupational wise distribution of the sample indicates that 53.61 per cent constitute agricultural group and the remaining 43.69 per cent belong to non-agriculture group. It is income which decides an individual's progress and prosperity in the society. Neo-literates are poverty stricken and they have poor income levels. The income levels of the sample reveal that 54.44 per cent are getting below Rs. 10,000 per year, and the remaining 45.56 per cent are getting Rs. 10,000 and above per year.

Literacy Achievement Among Neo-literates as Per NLM Norms

The implementation of total literacy campaign throughout the country has resulted in a good number of neo-literates emerging from the campaigns. What the neo-literates acquire in the centres is only fragile literacy and there is every possibility on the part of neo-literates in relapsing into illiteracy. Keeping this in view, an attempt has been made in the present study to know how many subjects are really literate through an achievement test as per National Literacy Mission Norms. The results are as follows:

Table 5.2 : Literacy attainment among the neo-literates

Category	Description	No	Percentage
1.	No. of learners attaining literacy skills as per norms (50 per cent of marks in 3 R's and aggregate of 70 and above)	228	63.33
2	No. of learners attaining 50.00 per cent of marks but not 70% on aggregate	69	19.17
3	No. of learners getting less than 50.00 per cent of marks in 3 R's	63	17.50
	Total	**360**	**100.00**

As Table 5.2 reveals 63.33 percent of the sample have achieved the literacy level as per norms. 19.16 percent of the sample have achieved 50 percent minimum marks in each of the sub-units of reading, writing and numeracy but could not get 70 percent marks on aggregate. 17.50 percent of the subjects could not quality in each of the sub-units of reading, writing and numeracy and the district administration has to pay attention on those who could not qualify as per norms (19.17+17.50 = 36.67 per cent).

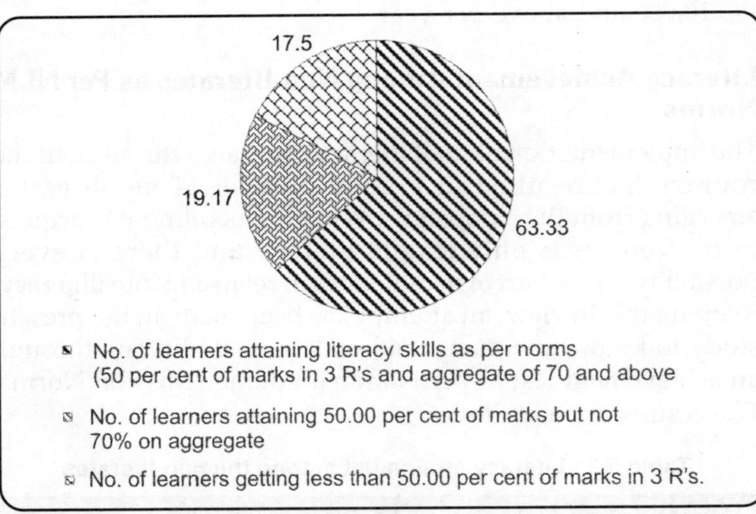

Fig. 5.1 : Pie-Diagram Showing the Literacy Attainment Among the Neo-Literates

Distribution of Performance Scores

The distribution of performance scores of neo-literates of the sample in reading, writing, numeracy and total achievement are as shown below:

The frequency distribution of achievement scores of neo-literates are as shown in Table 5.3. It can be observed from the table that the scores are more or less normally distributed. The mean, medium and mode of the distribution are 26.54, 26.77 and 27.23. The range of the achievement scores

Table 5.3 : Distribution of Achievement Scores in Reading

Class Interval	Frequency	Cumulative Frequency	Mid Point
12 – 16	10	10	14
16 – 20	38	48	18
20 – 24	62	110	22
24 – 28	101	211	26
28 – 32	96	307	30
32 – 36	38	345	34
36 – 40	15	360	38

in reading is 24, the lowest and highest scores being 13 and 37. The standard deviation and the quartile of the distribution are 4.92 and 4.17. The relationship between quartile deviation and standard deviation 2/3 standard deviation = Quartile deviation i.e., 2/3 (4.92) = 3.28 indicates that the distribution is slightly skewed. The skewness and kurtosis values of the

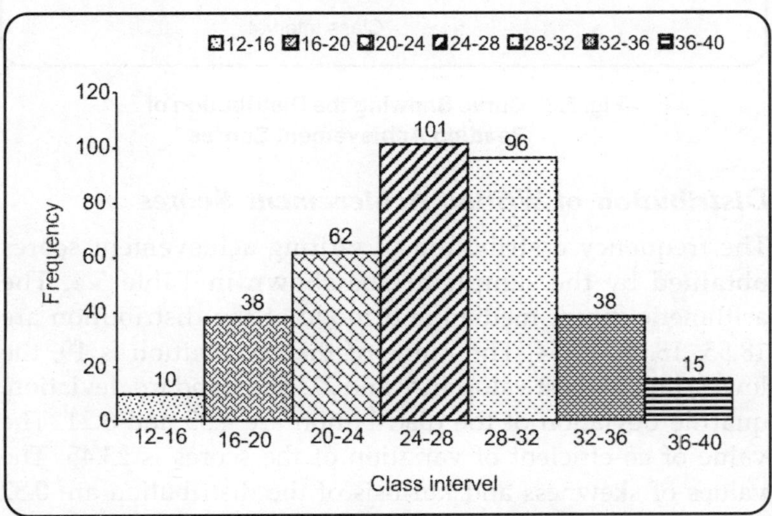

Fig. 5.2 : Histogram Showing the Distribution of Reading Achievement Scores

distribution are -0.14 and 4.08 whereas the co-efficient of variation is 18.53. The distribution is negatively skewed since mode is maximum and the value of arithmetic mean is the least. The value of median is less than mode but great than mean. The histogram and curve representing the reading achievement scores is presented (*See Fig. 5.2 on p. 101 and Fig. 5.3 below*):

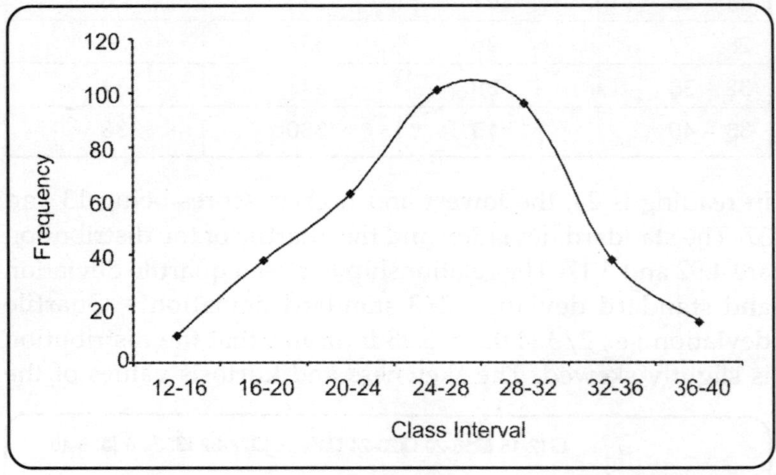

Fig. 5.3 : Curve Showing the Distribution of Reading Achievement Scores

Distribution of Writing Achievement Scores

The frequency distribution of writing achievement scores obtained by the sample are as shown in Table 5.4. The arithmetic mean, median and mode of the distribution are 18.55, 18.08, 17.54. The range of the distribution is 19, the lowest and highest value are 8 and 27. The standard deviation, quartile deviation of the distribution are 4.35 and 3.21. The value of co-efficient of variation of the scores is 23.45. The values of skewness and kurtosis of the distribution are 0.32 and 2.47. The distribution is positively skewed since mean is maximum and the value of mode is the least. The value of median is greater than the mode but less than the mean. Since the value of kurtosis is less than 3, the curve is less peaked than the normal curve i.e., platy kurtic. The histogram and the curve representing the distribution of writing achievement scores are presented (*Fig. 4 and 5*).

Table 5.4 : Distribution of Achievement Scores in Writing

Class Interval	Frequency	Cumulative Frequency	Mid Point
8 - 11	14	14	9.5
11 - 14	32	46	12.5
14 - 17	96	142	15.5
17 - 20	94	236	18.5
20 - 23	57	293	21.5
23 - 26	50	343	24.5
26 - 29	17	360	27.5

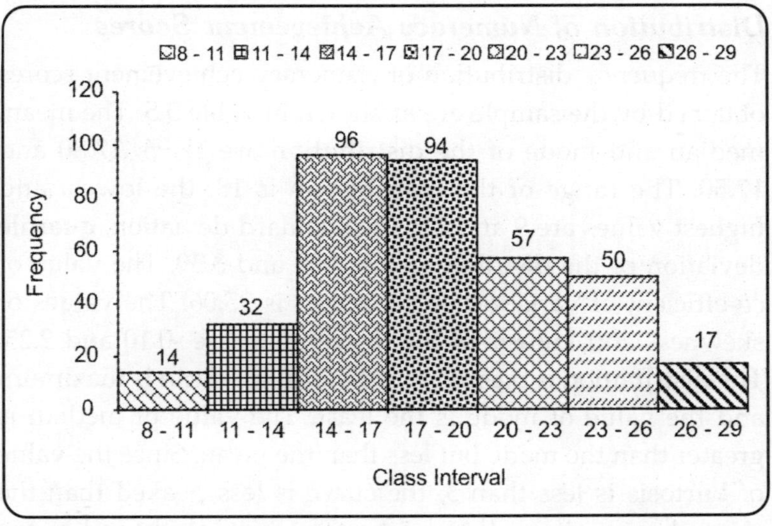

Fig. 5.4 : Histogram Showing te Distribution of Writing Achievement Scores

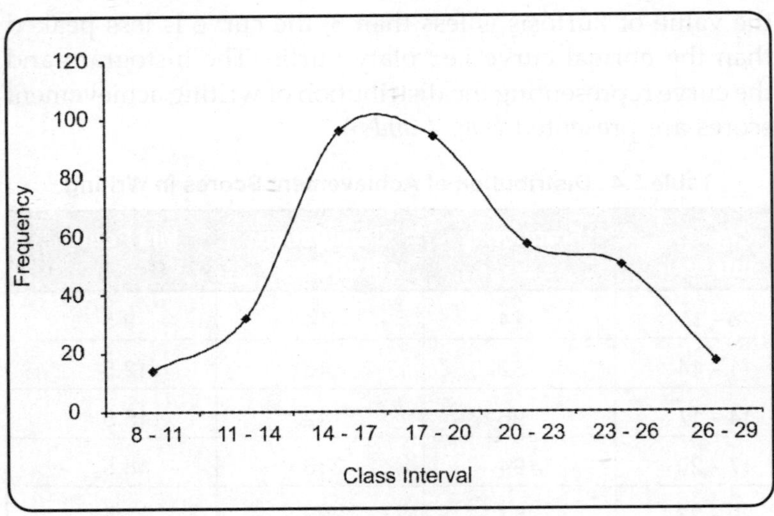

Fig. 5.5 : Curve showing the Distribution of Writing Achievement Scores

Distribution of Numeracy Achievement Scores

The frequency distribution of numeracy achievement scores obtained by the sample are as shown in Table 5.5. The mean, median and mode of the distribution are 17.95, 17.80 and 17.50. The range of the distribution is 18, the lowest and highest values are 9 and 27. The standard deviation, quartile deviation of the distribution are 4.50 and 3.39. The value of co-efficient of variation of the scores is 25.06. The values of skewness and kutosis of the distribution are -0.10 and 2.25. The distribution is positively skewed since mean is maximum and the value of mode is the least. The value of median is greater than the mode but less than the mean. Since the value of kurtosis is less than 3, the curve is less peaked than the normal curve i.e., platy kurtic. The histogram and curve representing the distribution of numeracy achievement scores are presented (Figs. 6 and 7).

Table 5.5 : Distribution of Achievement Scores in Numeracy

Class Interval	Frequency	Cumulative Frequency	Mid Point
7 – 10	14	14	8.5
10 – 13	36	50	11.5
13 – 16	71	121	14.5
16 – 19	98	219	17.5
19 – 22	62	281	20.5
22 – 25	59	340	23.5
25 – 28	20	360	26.5

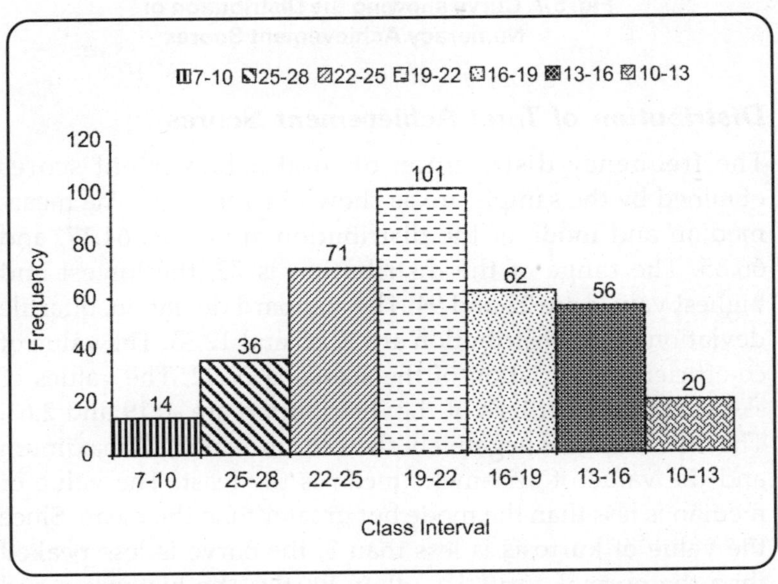

Fig. 5.6 : Histogram showing the Distribution of Numeracy Achievement Scores

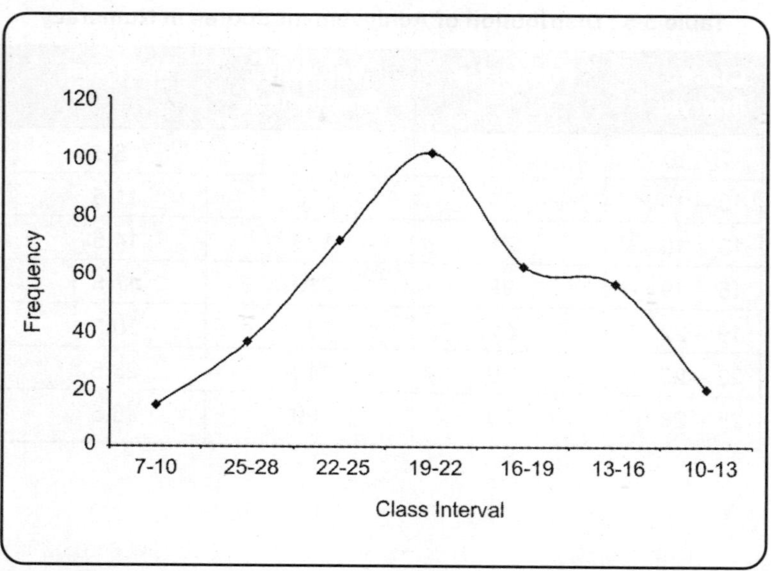

Fig. 5.7. Curve showing the Distribution of Numeracy Achievement Scores

Distribution of Total Achievement Scores

The frequency distribution of total achievement scores obtained by the sample are as shown in Table 5.6. The mean, median and mode of the distribution are 63.08, 64.17, and 66.35. The range of the distribution is 72, the lowest and highest values are 22 and 94. The standard deviation, quartile deviation of the distribution are 17.05 and 12.33. The value of co-efficient of variation of the scores is 27.02. The values of skewness and kurtosis of the distribution are -0.19 and 2.63. The distribution is negatively skewed since mode is maximum and the value of arithmetic mean is the least. The value of median is less than the mode but greater than the mean. Since the value of kurtosis is less than 3, the curve is less peaked than the normal curve i.e., platy kurtic. The histogram and the curve representing the distribution of total achievement scores are presented (Figs. 8 and 9).

Table 5.6 : Distribution of Total Achievement Scores

Class Interval	Frequency	Cumulative Frequency	Mid Point
20 – 30	9	9	25
30 – 40	32	41	35
40 – 50	45	86	45
50 – 60	51	137	55
60 – 70	103	240	65
70 – 80	55	295	75
80 – 90	48	343	85
90 – 100	17	360	95

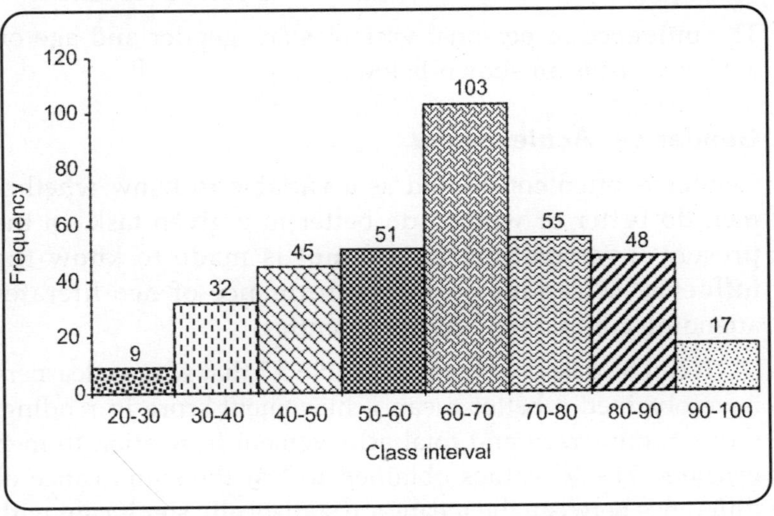

Fig. 5.8 : Histogram showing Distribution of Achievement Scores in Total Achievement

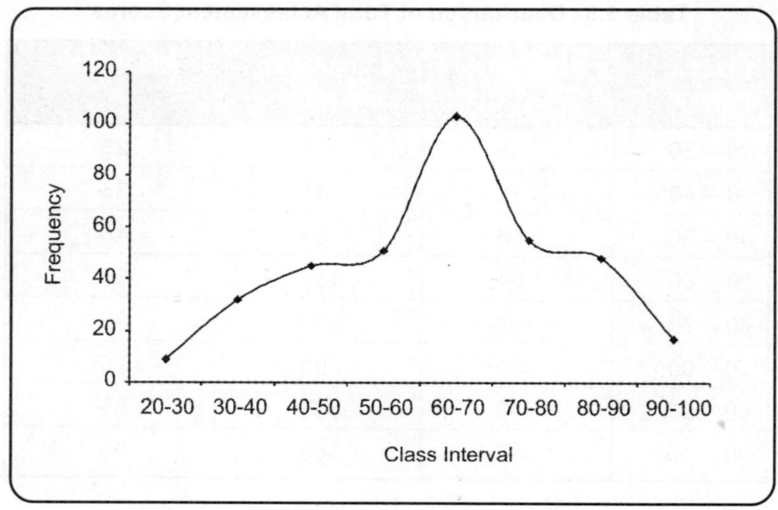

Fig. 5.9 : Curve showing the Distribution of Total Achievement Scores

Influence of Personal Variables on Achievement

The influence of personal variables *i.e.,* gender and age on achievement is an shown below:

Gender vs. Achievement

Gender is often considered as a variable to know whether men do better or women do better in a given task. In the present investigation, an attempt is made to know the influence of gender on the performance of neo-literates attending continuing education centres.

It can be observed from the Table 5.7 that women learners have obtained a better mean achievement score in reading, writing, numeracy and total achievement in relation to men learners. The 't' values obtained to test the significance of difference between the means are statistically significant with respect to reading, writing, numeracy and total achievement. Hence, the null hypothesis that 'Gender does not significantly influence the achievement of neo-literates in literacy skills and total achievement is rejected. The result are in line with the findings of Mathur (1976), Naik (1979), Salamathullah and Bareth (1984), Tribhuvan University (1982), Kulasekhar (2005).

Table 5.7 : Influence of Gender on Achievement

Group		N	Mean	Standard Deviation	't' value
Reading	Men	162	25.68	8.38	2.05*
	Women	198	27.40	7.51	
Writing	Men	162	17.09	5.37	5.22**
	Women	198	20.07	5.28	
Numeracy	Men	162	16.74	4.89	4.58**
	Women	198	19.17	5.32	
Total Achievement	Men	162	59.51	13.54	3.35**
	Women	198	66.64	15.59	

*Significant at 0.05 level

**Significant at 0.01 level.

Age vs. Achievement

Age is one of the biological factors. With age comes growth, intelligence and maturity. It is often observed that the performance of lower age group in performing physical and motor skills is better in relation to older age group. At times, in case of tasks requiring knowledge, skills, capabilities and experience older age group tend to perform better in relation to the younger age group. In a few occasions, age may not exert any significant influence on the performance of people. Keeping this in view, an attempt was made in the present study to know the influence of age on the achievement of neo-literates, the details of which are as shown in Table 5.8.

The neo-literates of the sample were divided into 3 groups in order to study whether there exists any significant difference in their achievement. A glance at the table 5.4

indicates that 15–25 years and 25–35 years age group have secured better a mean achievement score in relation to higher age group *i.e.,* 35 and above years. The mean differences in reading, writing, numeracy and total achievement are found to be statistically significant as 0.01 level. Hence, the null hypothesis that 'age does not significantly influence the achievement of neo-literates in literacy skills and total achievement' is rejected. The finding relating to age are similar to the findings of Pillai (1976), Vasudeva Rao (1988).

Table 5.8 : Influence of Age on Achievement

Area	N	Mean	S.D.	'F' value
Reading				
15-25 years	155	28.95	7.39	
25-35 years	90	26.21	6.67	10.37**
35 years & above	115	24.46	4.88	
Writing				
15-25 years	155	21.90	5.49	
25-35 years	90	17.85	5.20	8.63**
35 years and above	115	15.99	4.86	
Numeracy				
15-25 years	155	20.38	6.83	
25-35 years	90	17.65	5.31	9.72**
35 years & above	115	15.83	4.89	
Total achievement				
15-25 years	155	71.23	12.41	
25-35 years	90	61.71	15.20	6.74**
35 years & above	115	56.28	16.35	

**Significant at 0.01 level.

Influence of Social Variables on Achievment

The influence of social variables i.e., caste and marital status are as follows:

Influence of Caste on Achievement

Caste is one of the social variables which is often considerable by the researchers. In general there are three types of castes namely forward castes, backward castes, schedule castes and schedule tribes. The forward caste people due to their better socio-economic status and public relations are able to prosper

Table 5.9 : Influence of Caste on Achievement

Area	N	Mean	S.D.	't' value
Reading				
Forward	190	29.71	7.85	
Backward	121	26.76	8.67	8.45**
SC & ST	69	23.15	6.95	
Writing				
Forward	190	25.45	5.09	
Backward	121	17.65	4.91	17.67**
SC & ST	69	15.57	3.88	
Numeracy				
Forward	190	20.24	5.72	
Backward	121	17.94	4.28	8.18**
SC & ST	69	15.72	3.73	
Total achievement				
Forward	190	75.40	16.63	
Backward	121	62.35	12.47	11.79**
SC & ST	69	54.44	10.11	

** Significant at 0.01 level.

well in the society and the other communities are often having several problems like poverty, indebtness, lack of property, investment etc. Keeping this in view in the present study it was proposed to know whether neo-literates, representing various castes differ significantly in their performance or not. The details relating to the influence of caste on the achievement of neo-literates are as shown in Table 5.9.

It is clear from Table 5.9 that the learners belonging to forward communities have obtained better performance scores in relation to backward castes, schedule castes and schedule tribes. Further, the performance of backward castes is better when compared with the performance of schedule caste and schedule tribes in reading, writing, numeracy and total achievement. F test was employed to find out the significance of difference among the means and the calculated F values are found to be statistically significant at 0.01 level. Hence, the null hypothesis that 'caste doesn't significantly influence the achievement of neo-literates in literacy skills and total achievement' is rejected. The findings of the study are in line with in findings of Venkataiah (1978), Ramchandra (1995).

Marital Status vs. Achievement

In the present study, an attempt was made to find out the influence of marital status on the achievement of neo-literates, the details of which are as shown in Table 5.10.

The details as presented in Table 5.10 indicate that the married group of neo-literates have secured a mean reading achievement score of 28.00 with a standard deviation of 8.13. The mean reading achievement score of unmarried group is 25.08 with a standard deviation of 7.75. The 't' value calculated to find out the significance of difference between the means is statistically significant at 0.01 level. As far as the performance of neo-literates in writing is concerned the married group have secured a better mean performance score in relation to the unmarried group (20.25 > 16.91). The calculated 't' values

Table 5.10 : Influence of Marital Status on Achievement

Group		N	Mean	Standard Deviation	't' value
Reading	Married	240	28.00	8.13	3.79**
	Unmarried	120	25.08	7.75	
Writing	Married	240	20.25	5.30	14.28**
	Unmarried	120	16.91	4.53	
Numeracy	Married	240	19.52	4.71	5.53**
	Unmarried	120	16.41	3.95	
Total Achievement	Married	240	67.27	16.86	4.12**
	Unmarried	120	58.94	13.25	

**Significant at 0.01 level

of 14.28 is found to be statistically significant at 0.01 level. In the case of numeracy also married group have secured a slightly achievement score and the calculated t value of 5.53 is statistically significant are 0.01 level. A glance at the mean scores relating to total achievement indicate that the neo-literates representing the married group have secured a mean performance a score of 67.27 with a standard deviation of 16.86 and the neo-literates belonging to unmarried group have obtained a mean performance score of 58.94 with a standard deviation of 13.25, 't' test was employed to find out the significance of difference between the means and the obtained t value of 4.12 is found to be significant at 0.01 level. Hence the null hypothesis that "Marital status does not significantly influence the achievement of neo-literates in literacy skills and total achievement' is rejected. The studies by Kumaraswamy and Kulasekhar (2005), Rajendrudu (2005) have confirmed that marital status significantly influences the literacy performance of adult education participants.

Influence of Economic Variables on Achievement

The influence of economic variables i.e., occupation and Income on achievement of neo-literates is as follows:

Occupations vs. *Achievement*

In the present study, occupation of the neo-literates was considered in order to study its influence on achievement. The different types of occupations of neo-literates considered in the study are grouped under agriculture and non-agriculture.

Table 5.11: Influence of Occupation on Achievement

Group	N	Mean	S.D.	't' value
Reading				
Agriculture	193	27.08	7.80	1.12@
Non-Agriculture	167	28.05	8.49	
Writing				
Agriculture	193	18.46	5.81	0.44@
Non-Agriculture	167	18.70	4.73	
Numeracy				
Agriculture	193	17.82	5.79	0.51@
Non-Agriculture	167	18.09	4.52	
Total achievement				
Agriculture	193	63.37	16.54	0.53@
Non-Agriculture	167	64.84	19.28	

@ Not significant.

It can be observed from Table 5.11 that neo-literates belonging to non- agriculture group obtained a high mean achievement score in reading in relation to the group belonging to agriculture. The difference between the means is not statistically significant. With respect to writing skills low mean achievement score is secured by those belonging to agriculture in relation to non-agriculture group. However, the mean difference in writing scores between the groups is not statistically significant. As far as the influence of occupation on the performance of neo-literates on numeracy was concerned, a better mean achievement score was secured by the non-agriculture group when composed to agriculture group. The difference between the means is not statistically significant. When the mean total achievement scores are observed, a better mean score is obtained by those having non-agriculture as occupation in relation to agriculture group. The 't' value 0.53 indicates that there is no statistically significant difference between the means. Hence, the null hypothesis that occupation does not significantly influence the achievement of neo-literates in literacy skills and total achievement' is accepted.

Income vs. Achievement

It is income which decides the socio-economic status of the family. Since the neo-literates are belonging to lower income groups it was intended in the present study to know the influence of income if any, on their achievement. The neo-literates of the sample were divided into two income groups namely, low income group (Below Rs.10,000/- per year) and higher income group (Rs.10,000/- and above per year).

The details as presented in Table 5.12 indicate that a better mean performance score is obtained by higher income group Rs.10,000 and above per year in relation to the lower income group with respect to reading, writing, numeracy and total achievement scores. 't' test was employed to find out whether the two levels of income groups of neo-literates differ significantly in literacy skills or not.

Table 5.12 : Influence of Income on Achievement

Group		N	Mean	Standard Deviation	't' value
Reading	Below Rs. 10,000/- per year	196	25.33	7.83	3.36**
	Rs.10,000 & above per year	164	27.75	8.28	
Writing	Below Rs. 10,000/- per year	196	17.25	5.30	9.50**
	Rs.10,000 & above per year	164	19.91	4.85	
Numeracy	Below Rs. 10,000/- per year	196	17.02	3.94	10.76**
	Rs.10,000 & above per year	164	18.91	4.20	
Total Achievement	Below Rs. 10,000/- per year	196	59.60	17.63	3.27**
	Rs.10,000 & above per year	164	66.57	18.94	

**Significant at 0.01 level

The 't' values reveal that there exists statistically significantly difference with respect to reading, writing, numeracy and total achievement among the different income groups. Hence, the null hypothesis that 'Income does not significantly influence the achievement of neo-literates in literacy skills and total achievement' is rejected. The studies conducted by Ramachandra (1994), Vasudeva Rao (1988) indicated that higher the level of income better will be the performance of learners.

Influence of Personality Factors on Achievement

The influence of personality factors on the achievement of neo-literates is presented in Tables 5.13 - 5.28.

In the present study, an attempt is made to find out the influence of personality factors on the achievement of neo-literates. The learners of the study were divided into three groups possessing low, medium and high personality factor scores and their respective achievement scores were analysed. The learners were classified based on the criteria mean ± ½ standard deviation i.e., all the scores falling above mean + ½ standard deviation were classified as high group and similarly all the scores falling below mean – ½ standard deviation were classified as low group and the scores in between low and high groups were treated as medium group. A similar procedure was followed for all the 16 personality factors.

Table 5.13 : Influence of Factor A on Achievement

Group		N	Mean	Standard Deviation	't' value
Reading	High	91	27.34	8.44	4.01**
	Medium	145	26.62	8.30	
	Low	124	25.66	6.25	
Writing	High	91	19.34	5.76	4.47**
	Medium	145	18.81	4.38	
	Low	124	17.59	4.91	
Numeracy	High	91	19.94	5.13	5.03**
	Medium	145	17.62	3.81	
	Low	124	16.32	3.43	
Total achievement	High	91	66.22	13.93	5.29**
	Medium	145	61.83	11.25	
	Low	124	60.79	16.09	

Factor A vs. Achievement

The influence of Factor A on the achievement of neo-literates is as presented in Table 5.13. As can be seen from the Table 5.13 high scorers on the Factor A had better mean scores in reading, writing, arithmetic and total achievement than the low scorers on the factor. The differences between the mean scores of high medium and low groups in all achievement areas were statistically significant at 0.01 level.

A person who scores high on Factor A tends to be warm hearted and out-going type i.e., the person tends to be good natured, easy going, ready to cooperate, attentive to people, soft hearted, kindly, trustful and adaptable. He likes occupations dealing with people and socially impressive situations. He readily forms active groups. He will be generous in personal relations, less afraid of criticism, more able to remember the names of the people. In contrast, an individual who scores low on Factor A will be reserved and cool type. To elaborate, a person who scores low on Factor A tends to be shift, cool and aloof. He likes things rather than people, working alone and avoiding of clash of view points. He will be precise and rigid in his way of doing things and in personal standards. He may tend, at times, to be critical, obstructive or hard. Based on the description of characteristics it may be noted that stiff, cool, aloof and rigid nature of low scorers might have lowered their achievement in reading, writing and arithmetic skills in relation to high scorers.

Factor B vs. *Achievement*

Table 5.14 indicates the mean reading, writing, numeracy and total achievement scores along with respective standard deviations and F values obtained by the learners representing high, medium and low groups of the distribution of Factor B scores. As per the table, on all the four achievement ratings, neo-literates representing high group on the factor had better mean scores than the neo-literates representing medium and low groups. The mean differences between high and low scores in case of reading and writing are 4.26 and 2.61 points respectively. Similarly, the mean differences between of high, medium and low scores of numeracy and total achievement scores are 4.00 and 10.87 points respectively. The difference among the mean scores of the groups in all achievement areas are statistically significant at 0.01 level.

A person who scores high on Factor B tends to be quick grasper of ideas, fast learner and intelligent. He uses his

Table 5.14 : Influence of Factor B on Achievement

Group		N	Mean	Standard Deviation	't' value
Reading	High	83	28.25	8.53	5.86**
	Medium	153	27.38	7.75	
	Low	124	23.99	6.94	
Writing	High	83	20.10	5.59	6.02**
	Medium	153	18.17	4.85	
	Low	124	17.49	4.13	
Numeracy	High	83	20.40	5.18	7.47**
	Medium	153	17.09	3.10	
	Low	124	16.40	3.62	
Total achievement	High	83	68.75	18.88	16.28**
	Medium	153	62.64	14.68	
	Low	124	57.88	12.94	

insight and will be quick in adapting to circumstances. On the other hand, a person who scores low on Factor B tends to be slow to learn and grasp, dull and sluggish. He tends to have little taste or capacity for the higher forms of learning. As far as achievement in reading, writing and numeracy skills was concerned in order to achieve them quickly and effectively a person's quickness in grasping ideas, the fastness in his learning, the amount of interest he shows and his ability to adapt to the circumstances plays a vital role. On the other hand, slow grasping nature, dull and sluggish characteristics on the part of the neo-literates tend to hamper his academic achievement.

Factor C vs. Achievement

The mean reading, writing, numeracy and total achievement scores, standard deviations and respective F values obtained by the neo-literates representing high, medium and low groups of the distribution of Factor C scores are as indicated in Table 5.15. As can be seen from the table, the high scorers on the factor have marginally better mean scores in reading, writing, numeracy as well as total achievement than the low scorers on the factor. The differences in the means are not statistically significant at 0.05 level. However, based on the means it may be assumed that high scorers on the factor may be better achievers than low scorers.

Table 5.15 : Influence of Factor C on Achievement

Group		N	Mean	Standard Deviation	't' value
Reading	High	90	29.87	7.91	3.22@
	Medium	151	26.25	7.81	
	Low	119	23.52	7.50	
Writing	High	90	19.09	5.13	1.57@
	Medium	151	18.43	5.47	
	Low	119	18.22	4.51	
Numeracy	High	90	18.38	4.30	3.05@
	Medium	151	18.09	3.90	
	Low	119	17.41	3.31	
Total achievement	High	90	66.37	12.02	3.13@
	Medium	151	62.77	15.87	
	Low	119	60.12	18.05	

@ Not significant

A person who scores high on Factors C tends to be emotionally mature, stable, calm, pragmatic, realistic about life, placid and possesses ego strength. Further, he has the capacity to maintain high group morale. In contrast, a person who scores low on Factor C tends to be emotionally immature, easily perturbed, evasive of responsibilities, worrying and getting involved in unnecessary problem situations. For the purpose of better academic achievement we expect a neo-literate to be stable and calm in his nature and should have capacity to face the difficulties by realising the realities.

Possession of these qualities perhaps might have given an edge to the high scorers over low scorers on the factor to achieve better in reading, writing and numeracy units. Further, intolerance and worrying conditions in an individual may hamper his progress in academic achievement. The impact of these characteristics is noticed, though marginal in case of learners scoring low on the factor.

Factor E vs. Achievement

Table 5.16 shows the mean reading, writing, and total achievement scores, standard deviations and respective F values obtained by the neo-literates representing high, medium and low groups of the distribution of the Factor E scores. An examination of the results indicate that the differences between high, medium and low scores on the factor with reference to their achievement scores in reading, writing, numeracy and total achievement appear to be low

Table 5.16 : Influence of Factor E on Achievement

Group		N	Mean	Standard Deviation	't' value
Reading	High	120	25.11	8.29	2.26@
	Medium	121	26.26	7.83	
	Low	119	28.25	6.10	
Writing	High	120	18.10	5.67	0.55@
	Medium	121	18.27	4.26	
	Low	119	19.38	5.23	
Numeracy	High	120	17.36	4.17	1.26@
	Medium	121	18.08	4.23	
	Low	119	18.45	3.96	
Total achievement	High	120	60.57	13.39	2.18@
	Medium	121	62.61	14.81	
	Low	119	66.08	18.17	

@Not significant.

and they are not statistically significant at 0.05 level. On the whole, the trend of the means indicate that low scorers on the factor had better mean achievement scores than high scores on the factor.

A person who scores high on the factor tends to be ascendant, self-assured, assertive, independent minded and bold in his approach to situations. Further, he may at times be hard, stern, hostile, tough minded authoritarian in his approach. In contrast, a person who scores low on the factor tends to be a dependent, a follower and goes along with the groups. He tends to lean on others in making decisions and will be often soft hearted. He appears to be expressive and easily upset.

In order to improve reading, writing and numeracy skills the neo-literate should depend to an extent on his volunteer / prerak and follow his instructions carefully. Further, he has to observe the others and try to get the good points from them to improve his learning. He should be expressive in order to facilitate others to give necessary guidance to him in his learning. On the other hand, if the learner happens to be self assured, tough minded and authoritarian in his outlook, his learning will be hampered because of his over confidence and non-yielding nature to others suggestions. Perhaps these may be the reasons for the low scorers for having better achievement over the high scorers on the factor.

Factor F vs. *Achievement*

The mean reading, writing, numeracy and total achievement scores, standard deviations, and respective F values obtained by the neo-literates representing high, medium and low groups of the distribution of factor F scores are as shown in Table 5.17. As per the table, high scorers on the factor had better mean scores in reading, writing, numeracy and total achievement than the low scorers on the factor. F test was employed to find out the significance of difference among the means and the calculated F values are found to be statistically significant at 0.01 level.

Table 5.17: Influence of Factor F on Achievement

Group		N	Mean	Standard Deviation	'f' value
Reading	High	160	27.19	9.09	8.68**
	Medium	154	26.71	8.17	
	Low	46	25.92	7.44	
Writing	High	160	19.10	5.94	6.61**
	Medium	154	18.69	5.56	
	Low	46	17.85	3.99	
Numeracy	High	160	23.25	4.61	9.10**
	Medium	154	17.49	3.80	
	Low	46	13.25	3.49	
Total achievement	High	160	68.54	14.59	5.97**
	Medium	154	62.89	15.03	
	Low	46	56.82	18.31	

**Significant at 0.01 level

An individual who scores low on factor F tends to be taciturn, reticent, and introspective. Sometimes he will be incommunicative, pessimistic, anxious, depressed and slow. On the other hand, an individual who scores high on the factor tends to be cheerful, talkative, frank, expressive, quick, alert and unperturbable. Further, choice of elective leader frequently falls on him. An individual who is cheerful, talkative, frank, expressive, quick and alert in nature generally scores better than an individual who is introspective, incommunicative and slow in his approach. These may be the reasons for better mean scores in all the achievement areas for the high scorers on the factor than the low scorers.

Factor G vs. Achievement

The mean reading, writing, numeracy and total achievement scores, standard deviations and respective F values obtained by the neo-literates representing high, medium and low groups of the distribution of Factor G scores are as shown in Table 5.18. As can be seen from the table the mean reading, writing, numeracy and total achievement scores obtained by the high groups on the factor are higher to those achieved by low group on the factor. The trend of the mean achievement scores indicates better achievement on the part of high scorers on the factor and all the mean differences are statistically significant at 0.01 level. Based on the trend of the means it may be assumed that subjects scoring high on the factor will be better in their academic achievement than the subjects scoring low on the factor.

As per the description of the traits of Factor G, a person who scores high on the factor tends to be strong in character, responsible, determined, consistent, planful, energetic, cautious and well organised. Usually he will be cautious with

Table 5.18 : Influence of Factor G on Achievement

Group		N	Mean	Standard Deviation	'F' value
Reading	High	86	29.30	8.91	8.05**
	Medium	141	25.65	7.78	
	Low	133	24.69	5.21	
Writing	High	86	19.85	7.31	9.77**
	Medium	141	18.54	5.04	
	Low	133	17.25	4.73	
Numeracy	High	86	19.40	7.05	6.62**
	Medium	141	17.78	5.21	
	Low	133	16.70	4.95	
Total achievement	High	86	68.55	18.56	5.31**
	Medium	141	61.97	14.13	
	Low	133	58.64	12.55	

@ Not significant

high regard for moral standards and prefers efficient people to other companions. On the other hand, a person who scores low on the factor tends to be fickle, undependable, irresolute and unsteady. He is sometimes demanding, impatient, obstructive and lacks internal standards.

An adult learner who has keen desire to achieve literacy skills must feel responsible, determined and planful in his activities. Further, he should organise the issues around him so that they may not interfere with his regular learning. Since these traits coincide with the traits of high scorers on factor G, learners scoring high on the factor might have obtained better achievement scores than low scorers on the factor whose achievement might have been hampered by their impatient, unpredictable and unsteady nature.

Table 5.19 indicates the mean reading, writing, numeracy and total achievement scores, standard deviations and

Table 5.19: Influence of Factor H on Achievement

Group		N	Mean	Standard Deviation	'F' value
Reading	High	116	29.94	6.50	6.94**
	Medium	179	25.87	7.97	
	Low	65	23.83	7.71	
Writing	High	116	21.63	4.36	5.39**
	Medium	179	19.20	5.31	
	Low	65	14.63	4.67	
Numeracy	High	116	21.79	4.13	8.69**
	Medium	179	17.59	4.17	
	Low	65	14.50	3.93	
Total achievement	High	116	73.36	13.94	7.01**
	Medium	179	62.66	15.96	
	Low	65	53.26	17.79	

** Significant at 0.01 level

respective F values obtained by the neo-literates representing high, medium and low groups of the distribution of Factor H scores. As per the table, the high scorers on the factor had an edge over the low scorers in their mean achievement scores on all the ratings viz., reading, writing, numeracy and total achievement and differences among the means are statistically significant at 0.01 level. Based on the means it may be said that high scorers on the factor had better academic achievement than the low scorers.

A person who scores high on the Factor H tends to be sociable, adventurous, likes meeting people, active, responsive, friendly, impulsive, carefree and possesses capacity to face wear and tear in dealing with people and grueling emotional situations without fatigue. In contrast, a person who scores low on the factor tends to be shy, withdrawing, cautious and cool. Further, he tends to be slow and impeded in speed and in expressing himself. He prefers one or two close friends to large groups and will not be able to keep in contact with all that happens around him.

Characteristics like being active, impulsive, responsive, and ability to face wear and tear without fatigue, generally, may be helpful for an individual to score well in academic achievement. On the other hand, traits like withdrawing nature, shyness, restrained nature may hamper the academic achievement of the learners. These may perhaps be the reasons for better achievement scores to individuals scoring high on the factor than the low scorers on the factor.

The mean reading, writing, numeracy and total achievement scores, standard deviations and respective F values obtained by the neo-literates representing high, medium and low groups of the distribution of Factor I scores are as shown in Table 5.20. As per the description a person who scores high on Factor I tends to be tender minded, imaginative, introspective, artistic, fastidious and excitable.

Sometimes he will be demanding, impatient, dependent and impractical. He tends to slow up group performances and to upset group morale by negative remarks. In contrast, a person who scores low on the factor tends to be practical, realistic, masculine, independent, responsible and cultured. Sometimes he will be hard, cynical and smug. He tends to keep a group operating on a practical and realistic basis.

Table 5.20 : Influence of Factor I on Achievement

Group		N	Mean	Standard Deviation	't' value
Reading	High	119	25.05	7.90	0.09@
	Medium	121	26.48	8.25	
	Low	120	28.09	7.06	
Writing	High	119	18.13	5.14	0.11@
	Medium	121	18.25	5.71	
	Low	120	19.37	4.28	
Numeracy	High	119	17.44	4.26	0.85@
	Medium	121	18.15	4.18	
	Low	120	18.30	2.98	
Total achievement	High	119	60.62	16.22	0.07@
	Medium	121	62.89	15.20	
	Low	120	65.76	16.89	

@ Not significant

An examination of the results in the table indicates that low scorers on the factor had better mean achievement scores than the high scorers on the factor. The differences in the mean reading, writing, numeracy and total achievement scores of low, medium and high scorers on the factor are not statistically significant at 0.05 level.

Possession of traits like practical mindedness, realistic towards situations and feeling responsibility towards the work, practical and realistic approach might have helped low scorers on the factor to secure better achievement scorers. In case of neo-literates scoring high on the factor impractical characteristics possessed by them might be responsible for obtaining low achievement scores.

Factor L vs. Achievement

Table 5.21 indicates the mean reading, writing, numeracy and total achievement scores, standard deviations and respective F values obtained by the learners representing high, medium and low groups of the distribution of Factor L scores. As per the table, differences in the mean achievement scores for low and high scores on the factor are marginal. The mean reading, writing, numeracy and total achievement scores of high scorers on the factor were 25.74, 18.30, 17.45 and 61.49 respectively. The mean reading, writing, numeracy and total achievement of medium scores on the factor are 26.02, 18.55, 17.78 and 62.35. Similarly, the mean reading, writing,

Table 5.21 : Influence of Factor L on Achievement

Group		N	Mean	Standard Deviation	'F' value
Reading	High	119	25.74	6.29	0.73@
	Medium	171	26.02	7.17	
	Low	70	27.86	8.57	
Writing	High	119	18.30	5.51	0.22@
	Medium	171	18.55	4.13	
	Low	70	18.89	4.78	
Numeracy	High	119	17.45	4.11	2.36@
	Medium	171	17.78	4.24	
	Low	70	18.65	3.76	
Total achievement	High	119	61.49	16.22	1.15@
	Medium	171	62.35	15.20	
	Low	70	65.40	16.49	

@ Not significant

numeracy and total achievement of low scorers on the factor are 27.86, 18.89, 18.65 and 65.40 the differences among the means are not statistically significant.

As per the description of factor traits, an individual who scores low tends to be free of jealous tendencies, adaptable, cheerful, concerned about other people and a good team worker. On the other hand, an individual who scores high on the factor tends to be mistrusting and doubtful. Often he will be involved in his own ego, unconcerned about other people and a poor team worker.

Possession of traits like adaptability, cheerfulness, composedness and willingness to work in team might promote academic achievement of learners. On the other hand, mistrusting, and doubtful nature and possession of unwanted ego and not caring for people around might hamper the academic achievement of the neo-literates. These perhaps may be the reasons for differences that arised in the achievement of high, medium and low groups on the factor.

Factor M vs. Achievement

Table 5.22 indicates the mean reading, writing, numeracy and total achievement scores, standard deviations and respective F values obtained by the neo-literates representing high, medium and low groups of the distribution of Factor M scores. As per the manual description a person who scores high on the factor tends to be conventional, unconcerned, bohemian, ego-centric, sensitive and imaginative. He sometimes makes emotional scenes, is some what irresponsible, impractical and undependable. He is often rejected in group situations. In contrast, a person who scores low on the factor tends to be anxious to do the right thing, practical and conformist. An examination of the traits indicate that for better academic achievement characteristics like being anxious to do right things, practical and conformist nature may help the learners. On the other hand, unconventional, unconcerned and ego-centric characteristics expressed by neo-literates may hamper their academic achievement.

Table 5.22 : Influence of Factor M on Achievement

Group		N	Mean	Standard Deviation	't' value
Reading	High	127	25.92	8.19	0.12@
	Medium	179	26.15	8.23	
	Low	70	27.55	6.83	
Writing	High	127	17.35	5.32	0.32@
	Medium	179	18.58	4.45	
	Low	70	19.82	4.94	
Numeracy	High	127	17.34	3.35	0.05@
	Medium	179	18.15	4.22	
	Low	70	18.40	3.83	
Total achievement	High	127	60.61	16.27	0.10@
	Medium	179	62.88	16.79	
	Low	70	65.77	11.90	

@ Not significant.

Results in Table 5.22 indicate better mean reading, writing, numeracy and total achievement scores for low scorers on the factor than the high scorers. But, the differences between the means are very low and they are not statistically significant at 0.05 level. However, based on the trend of the means it may be assumed that low scorers on the factor may prove better than high scorers in obtaining achievement scores.

Factor N vs. Achievement

The mean reading, writing, numeracy and total achievement scores, standard deviations and respective F values obtained by the learners representing high, medium and low groups of the distribution of Factor N scores are as presented in Table 5.23. As per the table in all the sub-tests reading, writing, numeracy and total achievement the neo-literates representing high groups of the factor had better mean scores than the neo-literates representing low groups. The difference between the mean scores of high, medium and low groups are not statistically significant at 0.05 level. All these go to confirm that higher the score, on Factor N better will be the achievement of the neo-literates.

Table 5.23 : Influence of Factor N on Achievement

Group		N	Mean	Standard Deviation	'F' value
Reading	High	104	28.30	7.92	3.81@
	Medium	186	26.06	8.29	
	Low	70	25.27	6.43	
Writing	High	104	19.42	5.55	2.35@
	Medium	186	18.47	5.57	
	Low	70	17.85	4.84	
Numeracy	High	104	18.45	3.69	2.95@
	Medium	186	18.16	4.74	
	Low	70	17.29	3.92	
Total achievement	High	104	66.17	16.93	3.23@
	Medium	186	62.69	16.34	
	Low	70	60.41	14.94	

@Not significant

As per the description, an individual who scores low on Factor N tends to be unsophisticated, sentimental and simple. He is easily pleased and sometimes crude and awkward. On the other hand, an individual who scores high on the factor tends to be polished, experienced, worldly and shrewd. He tends to be hard hearted and analytical. He has an intellectual, unsentimental approach to situations. If a neo-literate possesses the characteristics attributed to high scorers on the factor, probably his achievement may be better compared to the one identified with traits of low scorers on the factor.

Table 5.24 : Influence of Factor O on Achievement

Group		N	Mean	Standard Deviation	't' value
Reading	High	84	24.60	7.50	3.51@
	Medium	137	25.92	8.17	
	Low	134	29.10	7.40	
Writing	High	84	18.20	5.33	0.84@
	Medium	137	18.25	4.77	
	Low	134	19.30	4.90	
Numeracy	High	84	17.22	4.15	1.99@
	Medium	137	18.28	4.06	
	Low	134	18.40	3.92	
Total achievement	High	84	60.02	15.76	3.08@
	Medium	137	62.45	16.61	
	Low	134	66.68	15.94	

Table 5.24 indicates the mean reading, writing, numeracy and total achievement scores, standard deviations, and respective F values obtained by the sample representing high, medium and low groups of the distribution of Factor O scores. As per the manual description a person who scores low on Factor O tends to be placid, calm with unshakable nerve. He has a mature, complete confidence in himself and in his capacity to deal with things. He will be realistic and secure. On the other hand, a person who scores high on the factor tends to be depressed, moody, a worrier, suspicious, broody and avoids people. He has a child like tendency to anxiety in difficulties. He does not feel accepted in groups or feel to participate. If a neo-literate possesses mature and complete confidence in himself and in his capacity to deal with things naturally his academic achievement will be better than the neo-literate who shows depressed, worried, suspicious, moody and grueling traits.

An examination of Table 5.24 indicates that the low scorers on the factor had better mean scores in reading, writing, numeracy and total achievement. However, the differences between the mean achievement scores of low, medium and high scorers on the factor are only marginal. Further, none of the differences are statistically significant at 0.05 level. On the whole, based on the trend of the means it may be concluded that lower the score for a learner on Factor O better will be his achievement in reading, writing and numeracy skills.

Factor Q_1 vs. Achievement

The mean reading, writing, numeracy and total achievement scores, standard deviations and respective F values obtained by the neo-literates representing high, medium and low groups of the distribution of Factor Q_1 scores are as shown in Table 5.25. As per the description, a person who scores low

Table 5.25 : Influence of Factor Q_1 on Achievement

Group		N	Mean	Standard Deviation	't' value
Reading	High	116	27.85	8.32	7.33**
	Medium	152	26.47	7.09	
	Low	92	25.31	6.87	
Writing	High	116	19.22	5.36	6.01**
	Medium	152	18.55	5.45	
	Low	92	17.97	4.36	
Numeracy	High	116	18.33	4.65	7.35**
	Medium	152	17.79	3.91	
	Low	92	17.77	4.01	
Total achievement	High	116	65.40	16.32	8.95**
	Medium	152	62.89	16.62	
	Low	92	60.99	15.77	

** Significant at 0.01 level.

on Factor Q_2 tends to be overly cautious and moderate. He will oppose any change, inclined to go along with tradition and tends not to be interested in analytical intellectual thought. On the other hand, a person who scores high On factor Q_1 tends to be interested in intellectual matters and fundamental issues. He frequently takes issues with ideas, either old or new. He tends to be more well informed, less inclined to moralize, and more inclined to experiment in life generally, and more tolerant of inconvenience. From the above description, it may be assumed that possession of attributes like interest in intellectual matters and fundamental issues and tolerance of inconvenience might help the learners to achieve better. An examination of the results in Table Q_1 indicates that on all the four achievement measures the high scorers on the factor secured better mean scores than the low scorers. All the mean differences between the high, medium and low scorers were statically significant at 0.01 level. Thus the trend of the significant differences indicate that better achievement goes with high scores on the factor.

Factor Q_2 vs. Achievement

The mean reading, writing, numeracy and total achievement scores, standard deviations and respective F values obtained by the neo-literates representing high, medium and low groups of the distribution of Factor Q_2 scores are as presented in Table 5.26. The mean reading, writing, numeracy and total achievement scores of high scorers on are low in all the cases. Further, none of the mean differences were statistically significant even at 0.05 level. However, the trend of the means indicate that low scorers on the factor had better performance than high scorers in their academic achievement.

As per the description, a person who scores low on the factor prefers to work and make decisions with other people and depends on social approval and admiration. He tends to go along with the group and may be lacking in resolution.

Table 5.26 : Influence of Factor Q_2 on Achievement

Group		N	Mean	Standard Deviation	't' value
Reading	High	96	25.40	8.07	1.99@
	Medium	145	26.86	7.93	
	Low	119	27.38	6.10	
Writing	High	96	18.11	4.25	1.90@
	Medium	145	18.15	5.80	
	Low	119	19.38	3.81	
Numeracy	High	96	17.16	3.84	1.64@
	Medium	145	17.30	4.15	
	Low	119	19.44	5.89	
Total achievement	High	96	60.67	16.41	2.91@
	Medium	145	62.31	16.30	
	Low	119	66.20	15.57	

@ Not significant

In contrast a person who scores high on the factor tends to be independent, resolute, accustomed to going in his own way, making decisions and taking action on his own. Craving for social approval and admiration and inclination to go along with a group may help a learner to achieve better than the learner who shows much independence and is in the habit of going in his own way. These may perhaps be the reasons for marginal superiority for the low scorers on the factor over the high scorers in their achievement scores.

Factor Q_3 vs. Achievement

Table 5.27 indicates the mean reading, writing, numeracy and total achievement scores, standard deviations and respective F values obtained by the neo-literates representing high, medium and low groups of the distribution of Factor Q_3 scores. As per the description of factor traits, a person who scores low on the factor tends to lack will control and character stability. He is not too considerate, careful or conscientious. In contrast, a person scoring high on the factor tends to have strong control of his emotions and general behaviour, is inclined to be considered, careful and possesses self-respect. From the description it can be assumed that controlling of emotions and showing carefulness in behaviour may be helpful to the learners to achieve better whereas lack of will control on the part of learners may hamper their academic achievement.

Table 5.27 : Influence of Factor Q_3 on Achievement

Group		N	Mean	Standard Deviation	't' value
Reading	High	159	27.95	8.86	2.97@
	Medium	118	25.88	8.33	
	Low	83	25.81	6.24	
Writing	High	159	19.10	4.46	3.32@
	Medium	118	18.26	5.82	
	Low	83	18.08	5.85	
Numeracy	High	159	18.74	3.97	1.43@
	Medium	118	18.63	4.24	
	Low	83	16.53	3.50	
Total achievement	High	159	65.79	17.30	3.11@
	Medium	118	62.77	16.34	
	Low	83	60.42	15.20	

@ Not significant.

An examination of the table indicates that high group on the factor had better mean achievement scores in reading, writing, arithmetic and total achievement than low group. However, the difference between the mean achievement scores of high, medium and low groups was marginal and none of the differences were statistically significant at 0.05 level. It can be concluded that high scorers on the factor had an edge over the low scorers in achieving reading, writing and numeracy skills.

Factor Q_4 vs. Achievement

The mean reading, writing, numeracy and total achievement scores, standard deviations and respective F values obtained by the neo-literates representing high, medium and low groups of the distribution of Factor Q_4 scores are as presented in Table 5.28. As per the table, the mean reading, writing, numeracy and total achievement scores of high group on the factor are low in all the cases. The differences between the mean achievement scores of high, medium and low groups on all the achievement scores are marginal and none of the differences are statistically significant at 0.05 level. However, based on the trend of the means it may be assumed that low scores on the factor facilitate better academic achievement.

Table 5.28 : Influence of Factor Q_4 on Achievement

Group		N	Mean	Standard Deviation	't' value
Reading	High	105	25.46	7.92	3.24@
	Medium	132	26.36	6.20	
	Low	123	27.80	6.80	
Writing	High	105	17.62	5.90	2.51@
	Medium	132	18.15	4.41	
	Low	123	19.98	3.72	
Numeracy	High	105	17.75	4.17	1.30@
	Medium	132	17.85	3.62	
	Low	123	18.30	3.98	
Total achievement	High	105	60.93	14.81	3.52@
	Medium	132	62.46	16.41	
	Low	123	66.08	17.16	

@ Not significant

As per the description of the factor traits, an individual who scores low on the factor tends to be calm, relaxed, composed and satisfied. In contrast, an individual who scores high on the factor tends to be tense, excitable, restless and impatient. He is often over fatigued. Further, he takes poor view of group unity, orderliness and leadership. If the learners possess majority of the traits attributed to the high scores on the factor, they may hamper their achievement. The trend of the mean achievement score, obtained by high and low scorers on the factor indicate the same.

Hence, the null hypothesis that 'Personality factors (as measured by Cattell's 16 PF) do not significantly influence the achievement of neo-literates and total achievement' is rejected with respect to variables A, B, F, G, H and Q_1 and accepted with respect to other variables (C, E, I, L, M, N, O, Q_2, Q_3, and Q_4).

Influence of Attitude on Achievement

Attitudes are pre-dispositions of people towards issues, objects and things. It is the attitude of the persons that determines his/her concern to involve in different situations. It is the attitude of neo-literates that decides to take part in programmes of adult and continuing education and to get benefited from them.

In the present study, an attempt is made to find out the influence of attitude on the achievement of neo-literates. The learners of the study were divided into three groups possessing high, medium and low attitude scores and their respective achievement scores were analysed. The learners were classified based on the criteria mean +_1/2 standard deviation i.e., all the scores falling above mean +1/2 standard deviation were classified as high group and similarly all the scores falling below mean -1/2 standard deviation were classified as low group. As per this criteria there were about 102 members in the high scoring group, 187 members in the medium scoring group and 71 members in the low scoring group. (vide table 5.29) The high scoring group on attitude have obtained a mean performance score of 30.48 in reading whereas the medium and low scoring groups on attitude have achieved mean reading performance scores of 27.51 and 21.63. The differences among the means were statistically significant at 0.01 level. The trend with respect to writing and numeracy scores also indicates that the low, medium and high scores on attitude have obtained achievement scores in a similar manner. The calculated 'F' values are also significant. As far as total achievement scores are concerned, the high scoring group on attitude have achieved a total performance score of 71.47 with a standard deviation of 20.03. Similarly, the medium scorers on attitude have achieved a mean total performance score of 64.21 with a standard deviation of 16.19. The low scorers on attitude have secured a total mean achievement score of 53.56

Table 5.29 : Influence of Attitude on achievement

Group		N	Mean	Standard Deviation	't' value
Reading	High	102	30.48	8.07	9.21**
	Medium	187	27.51	6.95	
	Low	71	21.63	5.37	
Writing	High	102	21.03	6.74	22.40**
	Medium	187	19.43	5.60	
	Low	71	15.28	4.57	
Numeracy	High	102	19.96	4.26	14.97**
	Medium	187	17.27	3.91	
	Low	71	16.65	4.80	
Total achievement	High	102	71.47	20.03	9.17**
	Medium	187	64.21	16.19	
	Low	71	53.56	10.28	

**Significant at 0.01 level

with a standard deviation of 10.28. The 'F' value of 9.17 calculated to find out the significance of difference among the means is found to be statistically significant at 0.01 level.

Hence, the null hypothesis that 'Attitude does not significantly influence the achievement of neo-literates in literacy skills and total achievement' is rejected.

Correlation Matrices

The simple correlations with dependent variables i.e., reading, writing, numeracy and total achievement are as shown in Tables 5.30-5.33 (*See pages 142 to 153*).

Correlation with Achievement in Reading

The order of 1-24 variables presented in the table are gender, age, caste, occupation, marital status, income, Factor A, Factor B, Factor C, Factor E, Factor F, Factor G, Factor H, Factor I, Factor L, Factor M, Factor N, Factor O, Factor Q_1, Factor Q_2, Factor Q_3, Factor Q_4, attitude and reading achievement (Table 28). The order of high correlations with reading achievement are as follows: Factor B (0.50), Attitude (0.45), Income (0.37), Caste (0.29), Factor Q_1 (0.25), Age (0.21), Factor A (0.21), Marital status (0.20), Factor E (0.18), Factor M (0.18), Factor Q_3 (0.18), Factor H (0.16), Factor F (0.15), Factor Q_2 (0.15), Factor N (0.13), Occupation (0.13), Gender (0.12), Factor C (0.12), Factor L (0.12), Factor G (0.11), Factor I (0.11), Factor Q_4 (0.08), Factor O (0.05).

Correlation with Achievement in Writing

The order of 1-24 variables presented in the table are gender, age, caste, occupation, marital status, income, Factor A, Factor B, Factor C, Factor E, Factor F, Factor G, Factor H, Factor I, Factor L, Factor M, Factor N, Factor O, Factor Q_1, Factor Q_2, Factor Q_3, Factor Q_4, attitude, and writing achievement (Table 29). The order of high correlation with writing achievement are as follows. Attitude (0.44), Age (0.35), Factor A (0.31),

Factor B (0.25), Caste (0.22), Factor I (0.22), Factor Q_1 (0.18), Income (0.16), Factor H (0.16), Factor F (0.15), Factor E (0.13), Factor C (0.12), Factor M (0.12), Factor O (0.12), Marital Status (0.11), Factor Q_2 (0.11), Gender (0.10), Occupation (0.08), Factor G (0.08), Factor N (0.08), Factor Q_3 (0.04), Factor L (0.02), Factor Q_4 (0.02).

Correlation with Achievement in Numeracy

The order of 1-24 variables presented in the table are gender, age, caste, occupation, marital status, income, Factor A, Factor B, Factor C, Factor E, Factor F, Factor G, Factor H, Factor I, Factor L, Factor M, Factor N, Factor O, Factor Q_1, Factor Q_2, Factor Q_3, Factor Q_4, attitude, and numeracy achievement (Table 32). The order of high correlation with numeracy achievement are as follows. Factor B (0.41), Attitude (0.38), Factor H (0.26), Marital status (0.24), Income (0.18), Factor F (0.18), Factor A (0.17), Factor Q_3 (0.17), Factor N (0.15), Factor I (0.14), Factor Q_2 (0.14), Caste (0.13), Factor E (0.13), Factor Q_4 (0.13), Occupation (0.12), Factor C (0.12), Factor O (0.12), Factor L (0.12), Factor M (0.11), Factor Q_1 (0.11), Age (0.08), Factor G (0.08) and Gender(0.05).

Correlation with Total Achievement

The order of 1-24 variables presented in the table are gender, age, caste, occupation, marital status, income, Factor A, Factor B, Factor C, Factor E, Factor F, Factor G, Factor H, Factor I, Factor L, Factor M, Factor N, Factor O, Factor Q_1, Factor Q_2, Factor Q_3, Factor Q_4, attitude and total achievement (Table 31). The order of high correlations with dependent variable are attitude (0.55), Factor B (0.50), Income (0.39), Factor N (0.39), Age (0.33), Marital status (0.28), Factor Q_1 (0.24), Factor Q_3 (0.24), Factor F (0.22), Factor C (0.18), Factor I (0.16), Factor G (0.15), Factor O (0.15), Factor H (0.14), Factor L (0.14), Caste (0.13), Factor E (0.13), Factor Q_4 (0.13), Occupation (0.12), Factor M (0.12), Gender (0.11), Factor A (0.11), Factor Q_2 (0.11).

Table 5.30 : Correlation Matrix of Reading Achievement

Sl.No.	1	2	3	4	5	6	7	8	9	10	11	12	13	14
1	1.00	0.22	0.02	-0.01	0.07	-0.16	-0.11	-0.01	-0.14	0.09	0.07	-0.02	-0.01	0.02
2		1.00	0.34	0.17	0.36	-0.71	-0.70	0.15	0.06	-0.08	-0.01	-0.01	0.01	0.06
3			1.00	0.07	0.38	-0.68	-0.73	0.23	-0.07	0.07	0.12	-0.13	0.01	0.01
4				1.00	-0.26	-0.07	-0.10	-0.17	0.15	0.10	-0.01	0.02	0.02	0.39
5					1.00	-0.50	-0.54	0.36	-0.01	-0.13	0.01	-0.02	0.02	0.18
6						1.00	0.91	-0.22	0.08	0.03	-0.07	0.07	-0.01	0.01
7							1.00	-0.28	0.04	0.04	-0.06	0.06	-0.01	0.02
8								1.00	-0.23	-0.02	0.01	-0.02	0.01	0.15
9									1.00	-0.16	-0.09	0.01	0.31	0.10
10										1.00	0.83	-0.15	0.22	0.62
11											1.00	-0.17	0.13	0.50
12												1.00	0.14	0.26
13													1.00	0.13
14														1.00

Sl.No.	15	16	17	18	19	20	21	22	23	24
1	0.05	0.09	-0.03	0.01	0.09	0.04	-0.15	0.07	0.10	0.12
2	-0.22	0.08	0.00	-0.02	0.17	-0.01	-0.17	-0.09	0.17	0.21
3	-0.33	0.01	0.01	-0.14	0.30	-0.13	-0.04	0.04	0.08	0.29
4	-0.17	-0.32	0.03	-0.04	0.06	0.20	-0.04	-0.29	0.16	0.13
5	-0.10	0.19	-0.01	-0.02	0.16	-0.25	-0.01	0.14	-0.03	0.20
6	0.35	-0.07	0.01	0.09	-0.27	0.11	0.10	0.02	-0.16	0.37
7	0.36	-0.05	-0.02	0.10	0.29	0.10	0.07	0.05	-0.15	0.21
8	-0.09	0.10	-0.02	-0.01	0.16	-0.11	-0.04	-0.02	-0.01	0.50
9	0.01	0.07	0.01	0.08	-0.21	0.03	0.11	-0.11	-0.01	0.12
10	0.50	-0.18	-0.02	0.15	0.17	0.20	-0.19	-0.10	0.09	0.18
11	0.48	-0.05	0.02	0.14	0.15	0.19	-0.22	0.09	-0.20	0.15
12	0.18	-0.39	0.42	0.25	-0.11	-0.32	0.57	0.20	-0.24	0.11
13	0.26	-0.31	0.40	0.71	0.22	-0.09	0.32	-0.24	-0.15	0.16
14	0.41	-0.09	-0.41	-0.05	0.09	0.33	-0.30	0.15	0.08	0.11
15	1.00	-0.15	-0.01	0.31	-0.05	-0.06	-0.06	0.08	0.07	0.12
16		1.00	-0.51	-0.15	0.15	0.14	-0.40	0.07	-0.09	0.18

Sl.No.	15	16	17	18	19	20	21	22	23	24
17			1.00	0.44	-0.11	-0.13	0.47	-0.09	-0.13	0.15
18				1.00	0.10	-0.08	0.24	-0.13	-0.01	0.05
19					1.00	0.13	-0.20	-0.01	0.05	0.25
20						1.00	-0.34	-0.05	-0.18	0.15
21							1.00	-0.18	0.17	0.18
22								1.00	0.26	0.08
23									1.00	0.45
24										1.00

1. Gender
2. Age.
3. Caste
4. Occupation
5. Marital Status
6. Income
7. Factor A
8. Factor B
9. Factor C
10. Factor E
11. Factor F
12. Factor G
13. Factor H
14. Factor I
15. Factor L
16. Factor M
17. Factor N
18. Factor O
19. Factor Q_1
20. Factor Q_2
21. Factor Q_3
22. Factor Q_4
23. Attitude
24. Reading achievement.

Table 5.31 : Correlation Matrix of Writing Achievement

Sl.No.	1	2	3	4	5	6	7	8	9	10	11	12	13
1	1.00	0.22	0.02	-0.01	0.07	-0.16	-0.11	-0.01	-0.14	0.09	0.07	-0.02	0.01
2		1.00	0.34	0.17	0.36	-0.71	-0.70	0.15	0.06	-0.08	-0.01	-0.01	0.01
3			1.00	0.07	0.38	-0.68	-0.73	0.23	-0.07	0.01	0.12	-0.13	0.01
4				1.00	-0.26	-0.07	-0.10	-0.17	0.15	0.10	-0.01	0.24	0.02
5					1.00	-0.51	-0.54	0.36	-0.01	-0.13	0.01	-0.02	0.02
6						1.00	0.91	-0.22	0.08	0.03	-0.07	0.07	0.01
7							1.00	-0.28	-0.04	0.04	-0.06	0.06	0.01
8								1.00	-0.23	-0.02	0.01	-0.02	0.01
9									1.00	-0.16	-0.09	0.01	0.01
10										1.00	-0.83	-0.15	0.31
11											1.00	-0.17	0.22
12												1.00	0.14
13													1.00

Sl.No.	14	15	16	17	18	19	20	21	22	23	24
1	0.02	0.05	0.09	0.01	0.03	0.09	0.04	-0.15	0.07	0.10	0.10
2	0.06	-0.22	0.08	-0.02	0.01	0.17	-0.15	-0.17	-0.09	0.17	0.35
3	0.01	-0.33	0.01	-0.14	0.01	0.30	-0.13	-0.04	0.04	0.08	0.22
4	0.39	-0.17	-0.32	-0.04	-0.40	0.06	0.20	-0.04	-0.29	0.16	0.08
5	-0.18	-0.11	0.19	-0.02	0.01	0.16	-0.25	-0.01	0.14	-0.03	0.11
6	0.01	0.35	-0.07	0.09	-0.01	-0.26	0.11	0.10	0.02	-0.16	0.16
7	-0.02	0.36	-0.05	0.10	0.01	-0.29	0.11	0.07	0.05	-0.15	0.31
8	-0.15	-0.10	0.10	-0.01	0.01	0.16	-0.11	-0.04	-0.02	-0.01	0.25
9	0.10	0.01	0.07	0.08	0.17	-0.20	0.03	0.11	-0.11	-0.01	0.12
10	0.62	0.50	-0.18	0.15	0.01	0.17	0.20	-0.19	-0.10	-0.04	0.13
11	0.50	0.48	0.05	0.14	0.01	0.15	0.19	-0.22	0.09	-0.15	0.15
12	-0.26	0.18	0.39	0.25	0.02	-0.11	-0.32	0.57	-0.20	-0.50	0.08
13	0.13	0.26	-0.31	0.71	0.42	0.22	-0.09	0.32	-0.24	-0.29	0.16
14	1.00	0.41	-0.09	-0.05	0.41	0.09	0.33	-0.30	-0.15	0.21	0.22
15		1.00	-0.15	0.31	-0.40	-0.05	-0.06	0.06	0.08	-0.19	0.02
16			1.00	0.45	-0.01	0.15	0.14	-0.47	0.07	0.34	0.12

Sl.No.	14	15	16	17	18	19	20	21	22	23	24
17				1.00	0.51	-0.10	-0.13	0.24	-0.09	-0.59	0.08
18					1.00	0.11	-0.08	-0.20	-0.13	0.31	0.12
19						1.00	0.13	-0.34	-0.01	0.44	0.18
20							1.00	0.35	-0.06	0.26	0.11
21								1.00	-0.18	-0.43	0.04
22									1.00	0.05	0.02
23										1.00	0.44
24											1.00

1. Gender
2. Age.
3. Caste
4. Occupation
5. Marital Status
6. Income
7. Factor A
8. Factor B
9. Factor C
10. Factor E
11. Factor F
12. Factor G
13. Factor H
14. Factor I
15. Factor L
16. Factor M
17. Factor N
18. Factor O
19. Factor Q_1
20. Factor Q_2
21. Factor Q_3
22. Factor Q_4
23. Attitude
24. Writing achievement

Table 5.32 : Correlation Matrix of Numeracy Achievement

Sl.No.	1	2	3	4	5	6	7	8	9	10	11	12	13
1	1.00	0.22	0.02	-0.01	0.07	-0.16	-0.11	-0.01	-0.14	0.09	0.07	-0.02	0.01
2		1.00	0.34	0.17	0.36	-0.71	-0.70	0.15	0.06	-0.08	-0.11	-0.01	0.01
3			1.00	0.07	0.38	-0.68	-0.73	0.23	-0.07	0.01	0.12	-0.13	0.01
4				1.00	-0.26	-0.07	-0.10	-0.17	0.15	0.10	-0.03	0.12	0.02
5					1.00	-0.50	-0.54	0.36	-0.01	-0.13	0.01	-0.02	0.02
6						1.00	0.91	-0.22	0.08	0.03	-0.07	0.07	0.01
7							1.00	-0.28	0.04	0.04	-0.06	0.06	0.01
8								1.00	-0.23	-0.02	0.01	-0.02	0.01
9									1.00	-0.16	-0.09	0.01	0.01
10										1.00	0.83	-0.15	0.31
11											1.00	0.17	0.21
12												1.00	0.13
13													1.00

Sl.No.	14	15	16	17	18	19	20	21	22	23	24
1	0.02	0.05	0.09	-0.03	0.01	0.09	0.04	-0.15	0.07	0.10	0.05
2	0.06	-0.22	0.08	0.00	-0.02	0.17	-0.01	0.17	-0.09	0.17	0.08
3	0.01	-0.33	0.01	0.01	-0.14	0.30	-0.13	0.04	0.04	0.08	0.13
4	0.39	-0.17	-0.32	0.03	-0.04	0.06	0.20	-0.04	-0.29	0.16	0.12
5	-0.18	-0.10	0.19	-0.01	-0.02	0.16	-0.25	0.01	0.14	-0.03	0.24
6	0.01	0.35	-0.07	0.01	0.09	-0.26	0.11	0.10	0.02	-0.16	0.18
7	-0.02	-0.09	-0.05	-0.02	0.10	-0.29	0.10	0.07	0.05	-0.15	0.17
8	-0.15	0.01	0.10	-0.02	-0.01	0.16	-0.11	-0.04	-0.05	-0.01	0.41
9	0.10	0.50	0.07	0.01	0.08	-0.20	0.03	0.11	-0.02	-0.01	0.12
10	0.62	0.48	-0.18	-0.02	0.15	0.17	0.20	-0.19	-0.11	-0.04	0.13
11	0.50	0.18	-0.05	0.02	0.14	0.15	0.19	-0.22	-0.10	-0.15	0.18
12	-0.26	0.26	-0.39	0.42	0.25	-0.11	-0.32	0.57	0.09	-0.50	0.08
13	0.13	0.41	-0.34	0.40	0.71	0.22	-0.09	0.32	0.20	-0.29	0.26
14	1.00	0.44	0.31	-0.41	-0.05	0.09	0.33	-0.30	0.24	0.21	0.14
15		1.00	0.16	-0.04	0.31	-0.05	-0.06	-0.06	-0.15	-0.19	0.12
16			1.00	0.51	-0.15	0.05	0.14	-0.40	0.08	0.34	0.11

Sl.No.	14	15	16	17	18	19	20	21	22	23	24
17				1.00	0.44	-0.11	-0.13	0.47	0.07	-0.59	0.15
18					1.00	0.10	-0.08	0.24	-0.09	-0.31	0.12
19						1.00	0.13	-0.20	-0.13	0.44	0.11
20							1.00	-0.34	-0.01	0.26	0.14
21								1.00	-0.05	-0.43	0.17
22									1.00	0.05	0.13
23										1.00	0.38
24											1.00

1. Gender
2. Age.
3. Caste
4. Occupation
5. Marital Status
6. Income
7. Factor A
8. Factor B
9. Factor C
10. Factor E
11. Factor F
12. Factor G
13. Factor H
14. Factor I
15. Factor L
16. Factor M
17. Factor N
18. Factor O
19. Factor Q_1
20. Factor Q_2
21. Factor Q_3
22. Factor Q_4
23. Attitude
24. Nemeracy achievement.

Table 5.33 : Correlation Matrix of Total Achievement

Sl.No.	1	2	3	4	5	6	7	8	9	10	11	12	13	14
1	1.00	0.22	0.02	-0.01	0.07	-0.16	-0.11	-0.01	-0.14	0.09	0.07	-0.02	-0.01	0.02
2		1.00	0.34	0.17	0.36	-0.71	-0.70	0.15	0.06	-0.08	-0.01	-0.01	0.01	0.06
3			1.00	0.07	0.38	-0.68	-0.73	0.23	-0.01	0.01	0.12	-0.13	0.01	0.01
4				1.00	0.26	-0.07	-0.10	-0.17	0.15	0.10	-0.01	0.02	0.02	0.39
5					1.00	-0.50	-0.54	0.36	-0.01	-0.13	0.01	-0.02	0.02	0.18
6						1.00	0.91	-0.22	0.08	0.03	-0.07	0.07	-0.01	0.01
7							1.00	-0.28	0.04	0.04	-0.06	0.06	-0.01	0.02
8								1.00	-0.23	-0.02	0.01	-0.02	0.01	0.15
9									1.00	-0.16	-0.09	0.01	0.01	0.10
10										1.00	0.83	-0.15	0.31	0.62
11											1.00	-0.17	0.21	0.50
12												1.00	0.13	0.26
13													1.00	0.13
14														1.00

Sl.No.	15	16	17	18	19	20	21	22	23	24
1	0.05	0.09	-0.03	0.01	0.09	0.04	-0.15	0.07	0.10	0.11
2	-0.22	0.08	0.00	-0.02	0.17	-0.01	-0.17	-0.09	0.17	0.33
3	-0.33	0.01	0.01	-0.14	0.30	-0.13	-0.04	0.04	0.08	0.13
4	-0.17	-0.32	0.03	-0.04	0.06	0.20	-0.04	-0.29	0.16	0.12
5	-0.10	0.19	-0.01	-0.02	0.16	-0.25	-0.01	0.14	-0.03	0.28
6	0.35	-0.07	0.01	0.09	-0.26	0.11	0.10	0.02	-0.16	0.39
7	0.36	-0.05	-0.02	0.10	-0.29	0.10	0.07	0.05	-0.15	0.11
8	-0.09	0.10	-0.02	-0.01	0.16	-0.11	-0.04	-0.02	-0.01	0.50
9	0.01	0.07	0.01	0.08	-0.20	0.03	0.11	-0.11	-0.02	0.18
10	0.50	-0.18	-0.02	0.15	0.17	0.20	-0.19	-0.10	-0.04	0.13
11	0.48	-0.05	0.02	0.14	0.15	0.19	-0.22	0.09	-0.15	0.22
12	0.18	-0.39	0.42	0.25	-0.11	-0.32	0.57	-0.20	-0.50	0.15
13	0.26	-0.31	0.41	0.71	0.22	-0.09	0.32	-0.24	-0.29	0.14
14	0.41	0.09	-0.40	-0.05	0.09	0.33	-0.30	-0.15	0.22	0.16
15	1.00	-0.15	-0.01	0.31	-0.05	-0.06	-0.06	0.08	-0.19	0.14
16		1.00	-0.51	-0.15	0.15	0.14	-0.40	0.07	0.34	0.12

Sl.No.	15	16	17	18	19	20	21	22	23	24
17			1.00	0.44	-0.10	-0.13	0.47	-0.09	-0.59	0.39
18				1.00	0.11	-0.08	0.24	-0.13	-0.31	0.15
19					1.00	0.13	-0.20	-0.01	0.44	0.24
20						1.00	-0.34	-0.05	0.26	0.11
21							1.00	-0.18	-0.43	0.24
22								1.00	0.05	0.13
23									1.00	0.55
24										1.00

1. Gender
2. Age
3. Caste
4. Occupation
5. Marital Status
6. Income
7. Factor A
8. Factor B
9. Factor C
10. Factor E
11. Factor F
12. Factor G
13. Factor H
14. Factor I
15. Factor L
16. Factor M
17. Factor N
18. Factor O
19. Factor Q_1
20. Factor Q_2
21. Factor Q_3
22. Factor Q_4
23. Attitude
24. Total achievement

Multiple Regression Analysis

Multiple regression analysis is a technique to study the effects and magnitudes of more than one independent variable using principles of correlation and regression. This helps to segregate the factors that significantly influence the dependent variable. Since achievement of neo-literates is influenced by the simultaneous operation of a wide range of factors at a given point of time, the relative contribution of each of these factors in explaining the performance of neo-literates cannot be assessed correctly unless they are examined together. Hence, multiple regression analysis was utilised to estimate the percentage of variance in the achievement of neo-literates as explained by each one of the independent variables.

Factors Predicting Achievement of Neo-literates in Reading

Detailed presentation of the stepwise regression analysis on achievement of neo-literates in reading is as shown in Table 5.34. Out of 23 independent variable considered for analysis i.e., gender, age, caste, occupation, marital status, income, Factor A, Factor B, Factor C, Factor E, Factor F, Factor G, Factor H, Factor I, Factor L, Factor M, Factor N, Factor O, Factor Q_1, Factor Q_2, Factor Q_3, Factor Q_4, attitude only 6 variables were significantly related and explained 42.72 per cent of variance in the reading achievement. It may be seen from the table that the first variable that entered into the stepwise multiple regression analysis is that Factor B. The multiple correlation R^3 is 0.50 which is nothing but simple correlation shown in Col. 11 between the dependent variable, 'achievement in reading' and the most influencing variable Factor B. The value indicated that the strength of the relationship between the two as 10.66 (vide col. 7). It may be observed that 'R' was significant at 0.01 level (119.45 for 1 and 358 degrees of freedom) (vide col.6). The co-efficient of multiple determination R^2 disclosed that about 25 per cent of

Table 5.34 : Factors significantly influencing Neo-literates Achievement in Reading as denoted by proportion of variance explained (R^2) by multiple Regression Analysis.

Step No.	Independent variable entered in each step	Multiple correlation R	R^2	Standard error of multiple estimate	F-value (d.f) and level of signifi-cance	B-co-efficient or B-partial regression co-efficient	t-value for B and level of signifi-cance	Constant	B-Beta co-efficient	Simple correla-tion co-efficient with depen-dent	Percentage of variance explained by each indepen-dent variable
1	2	3	4	5	6	7	8	9	10	11	12
1	Factor B	0.50	0.25	10.60	119.45	10.66	10.93	27.42	0.50	0.50	25.02
					(1,358)						
2	Attitude	0.55	0.30	12.39	78.69	12.66	9.32	29.11	0.42	0.45	21.46
					(2,357)	7.04	5.36		0.25		9.13
3	Income	0.58	0.34	12.77	62.29	10.46	10.20	33.41	0.46	0.37	23.17
					(3,356)	9.28	5.33		0.23		8.84
						7.39	4.56		0.19		2.41
4	Caste	0.60	0.36	14.85	51.95	10.11	4.57	37.72	0.29	0.29	14.59
					(4,355)	8.38	5.29		0.23		8.62
						5.13	4.35		0.18		2.26
						4.03	3.75		0.23		11.43

1	2	3	4	5	6	7	8	9	10	11	12
5	Factor Q_1	0.63	0.39	12.71	49.93	3.36	4.04	44.43	0.25	0.25	12.75
					(5,354)	4.56	5.57		0.24		8.90
						2.12	4.44		0.18		2.26
						2.21	4.16		0.25		12.46
						3.20	3.85		0.17		3.48
6	Age	0.65	0.42	11.52	43.92	-2.93	3.57	38.52	0.22	0.21	11.10
					(6,353)	-5.39	6.58		0.28	0.28	10.61
						1.66	3.48		0.14	0.14	1.78
						-2.41	4.63		0.27	0.27	10.59
						3.75	4.91		0.20	0.20	4.08
						-3.31	4.21		0.18	0.18	4.56

variance (vide col.8) in the reading achievement was accounted by Factor B. The standard error of multiple estimate (col.5) (10.60) revealed that nearly 68 per cent of the obtained achievement scores were within the range of ± 10.60 point of predicted achievement scores in reading. The partial regression co-efficient or β co-efficient presented in col.10 was 0.50. The constant value that would be considered in the equation at the end of the first step with which the prediction of achievement in reading would be possible is as shown in col.9. The general form of the prediction equation may be given as:

$$x^2 = a + b_1 x_1 + b_2 x_2 + b_3 x_3 + \ldots\ldots. + b_n x_n$$

Where x^1 denotes the predicted score of the dependent variable. A is the constant, b_1, b_2, b_3 ..... b_n are partial regression co-efficient and x_1, x_2, x_3...... x_n are obtained values on different independent variables. Thus, the actual equation at the end of the first step would be:

Reading achievement = 27.42 + 10.66 (Factor B) .... *(1.1)*

The second variable that entered into the stepwise regression analysis was Attitude. The multiple correlation obtained between achievement in reading and the two independent variable namely. Factor B and Attitude was 0.55 per cent (col.3). Thus, the strength of the relationship between reading achievement and the two independent variables put together was 55 per cent. The relationship was significant at 0.01 level as the 'F' value 78.69 was far beyond the table value for 2 and 357 degrees of freedom. The two variable put together could explain about 30.59 per cent (R^2 = 0.30) of the variance in the dependent variable i.e., reading achievement. The standard error of multiple estimate (SE of R) in col.5 revealed that merely 68 per cent of the obtained reading achievement scores would be within the range of ± 12.39 (col.5) points of predicted reading achievement. The partial regression co-efficient shown in col.7 disclosed that when Factor B and attitude were included as predictor variables achievement of neo-literates in reading would increase by 12.66 and 7.84 points for every unit of increase in Factor B and attitude respectively. Both the partial regression co-efficients ('t' values) were significant at 0.01 level as shown in col.8. The regression equation to predict achievement in reading with Factor B and attitude as predictor variables was

Reading Achievement = *29.11 + 12.66 (Factor B) + 7.84 (Attitude)* ...(1.2)

In the hierarchy of predictor variables associated with reading achievement of learners 'income' entered as the next important variable. The multiple correlation of the combined association of Factor B, attitude and income 0.58 (col.3) was significant at 0.01 level ('F' = 62.29 for 3 and 356 degrees of freedom). The value of R^2 (0.34) (Col.4) disclosed that about 34 per cent of variance in reading achievement was explained by these three variables. Out of this variance 23.17 per cent was explained by Factor B, 8.84 per cent by attitude and 2.41 per cent by income. When the three predictor variables were considered the partial regression co-efficients (col.7) indicated that the increase in reading achievement was 10.46, 9.28 and 7.39 units for every unit increase in Factor B, attitude and income. The three 't' values obtained were significant at 0.01 level. The regression equation at this step with constant 33.41 was

Reading achievement = *33.41 + 10.46 (Factor B) + 9.28 (Attitude) + 7.39 (income)* .... *(1.3)*

The next variable that entered into the step wise regression analysis was caste. The multiple R was 0.60. The 'F' value obtained (51.95 for 4 and 355 degrees of freedom) was significant beyond 0.01 level. The value of R^2 (0.36) revealed that the combined strength of relationship between Factor B, attitude, income, caste and the dependent variable reading achievement was 36 per cent. The contribution of each of the predictor variables was 14.59, 8.62, 2.26 and 11.43 per cent by the variables namely, Factor B, attitude, income, and caste respectively. The standard error of multiple estimate indicated that 68 per cent of the obtained reading achievement scores would be without the range of ± 14.85 points (col.5) units of predicted scores of achievement. The partial regression co-efficient (col.7) disclosed that when the four variables namely, Factor B, attitude, income and caste were included in the regression analysis, the reading achievement would increase by 10.11, 8.38, 5.13 and 4.03 units for every unit increase in the 4 variables respectively. The regression co-efficient which would predict reading achievement was

Reading Achievement = *37.72 + 10.11 (Factor B) + 8.38 (Attitude) 5.13 (income) + 4.03 (Caste)* ... *(1.4)*

The next variable that entered the stepwise regression analysis was factor Q_1 (intelligence).The multiple correlation obtained between reading achievement and the independent variables namely, Factor B, attitude, income, caste and Factor Q_1 was 0.63. The relationship was significant as 0.01 level as the F value of 49.93 for 5 and 354 degrees of freedom was for beyond the table value. The five variables put together explained about 39 per cent of the variance in the reading achievement of the learners. The standard errors of multiple estimate revealed that 68 per cent of the obtained achievement scores would be within the range of ±12.71 units of the predicted scores. The regression equation with the constant 44.43 was

Reading achievement = *44.43 + 13.66 (Factor B) + 4.36 (Attitude) + 2.12 (income) + 2.21(caste) + 3.20 (factor* Q_1*)* ....*(1.5)*

The next variable that entered into the stepwise regression analysis was 'age'. The 'F' value obtained 43.92 (for 6 and 356 degrees of freedom) was significant beyond 0.01 level. The value of R_2 (0.42) revealed that the combined strength of the relationship between Factor B, attitude, income, caste, factor Q_1 and age and the dependent variable reading achievement was 42.00 percent. The contribution of each of the predictor variables was Factor B (11.10 percent), attitude (10.61 percent), income (10.78 percent), caste (10.50 percent), Factor Q_1 (4.08 percent) and age (4.56 percent).

Thus, out of 23 independent variable namely, gender, age, caste, occupation, marital status, income, Factor A, Factor B, Factor C, Factor E, Factor F, Factor G, Factor H, Factor I, Factor L, Factor M, Factor N, Factor O, Factor Q_1, Factor Q_2, Factor Q_3, Factor Q_4, attitude only 6 variables entered the regression analysis. In brief, the variance explained by the six variables was as follows:

Sl. No.	Independent Variable	Percentage of variance explained
1	Factor B	11.10
2	Attitude	10.61
3	Income	1.78
4	Caste	10.59
5	Factor Q_1	4.08
6	Age	4.56
	Total	**42.72**

Hence, the null hypothesis that 'No single variable or a set of variables included in the study do not significantly exert their contribution to reading achievement of neo-literates' is rejected except in case of variables *viz.*, Factor B, Attitude, income, caste, Factor Q_1 and age.

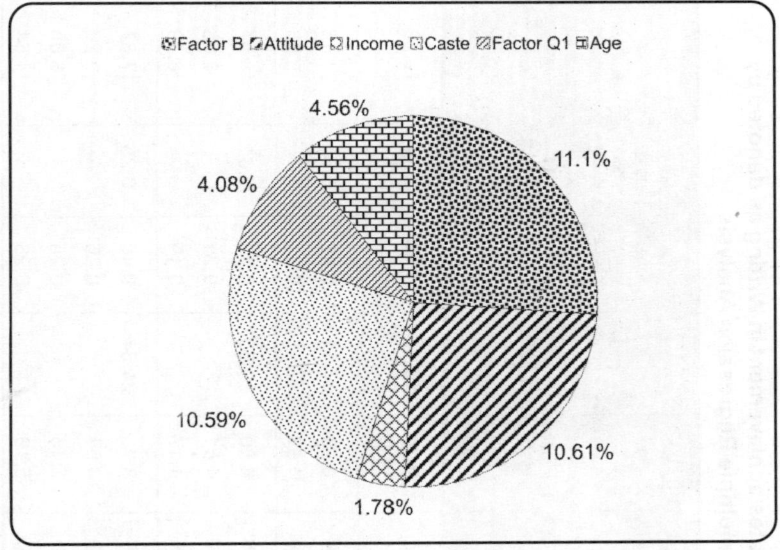

Fig. 5.10 : Percentage of Variance Explained by Independent variables on Reading Achievement

Factors Predicting Achievement of Neo-literates in Writing

Detailed analysis of the stepwise regression analysis on achievement of neo-literates in writing is shown in Table 5.35. Out of 23 independent variables considered for analysis i.e., gender, age, caste, occupation, marital status, income, Factor A, Factor B, Factor C, Factor E, Factor F, Factor G, Factor H, Factor I, Factor L, Factor M, Factor N, Factor O, Factor Q_1, Factor Q_2, Factor Q_3, Factor Q_4, attitude only 6 variables were significantly related and explained 38.26 per cent of variance in the writing achievement of neo-literates. It may be seen from the table that the first variable that entered in to the stepwise multiple regression analysis is attitude. The multiple correlation R (col.3) is 0.44 which is nothing but simple correlation shown in col. 11 between the dependent variable 'achievement in writing' and the most influencing variable attitude. The value indicated that the strength of the

Table 5.35 : Factors significantly influencing Neo-literates achievement in Writing as denoted by proportion of variance explained (R^2) by multiple Regression Analysis

Step No.	Independent variable entered in each step	Multiple correlation R	R^2	Standard error of multiple estimate	F-value (d.f) and level of significance	B-co-efficient or B-partial regression co-efficient	t-value for B and level of significance	Constant	B-Beta co-efficient	Simple correlation co-efficient with dependent	Percentage of variance explained by each independent variable
1	2	3	4	5	6	7	8	9	10	11	12
1	Attitude	0.44	0.19	12.44	87.18	14.12	9.34	15.17	0.44	0.44	19.58
					(1.358)						
2	Age	0.49	0.24	13.98	57.03	8.44	10.23	17.11	0.47	0.35	21.13
					(2,357)	7.78	4.67		-0.21		3.08
3	Factor A	0.52	0.27	10.66	45.57	6.66	8.80	19.50	0.41	0.31	18.57
					(3,356)	4.37	4.61		-0.21		2.98
						4.95	4.17		-0.19		6.19
4	Factor B	0.57	0.32	8.74	43.41	8.76	8.75	24.54	0.40	0.25	17.87
					(4.355)	4.29	3.54		-0.16		2.26
						3.40	5.46		-0.25		8.06
						3.06	5.19		-0.23		4.64

1	2	3	4	5	6	7	8	9	10	11	12
5	Caste	0.59	0.35	6.95	39.58	8.74	8.91	28.99	0.40	0.22	17.80
					(5,354)	7.78	4.74		-0.22		3.13
						5.41	5.60		-0.25		8.09
						3.21	5.41		-0.24		4.73
						4.57	4.08		-0.18		2.09
6	Factor Q_1	0.61	0.38	5.21	36.49	8.54	8.51	33.15	0.38	0.18	16.85
						6.71	4.63		-0.21		3.01
						5.59	5.99		-0.27		8.53
						3.46	6.03		-0.26		5.25
						1.48	3.90		-0.17		1.97
						2.07	3.72		-0.15		2.65

relationship between the two 14.12 (vide col.7). It may be observed that 'R' was significant at 0.01 level (87.18 for and 358 degrees of freedom) (vide col.6). The co-efficient of multiple determination R_2 disclosed that about 19 per cent of variance (vide col.3) in the writing achievement was accounted by attitude. The standard error of multiple estimate (col.5) 12.44 revealed that nearly 68 per cent of the obtained scores within the range of ± 12.44 points of predicted writing achievement scores. The partial regression co-efficient or b co-efficient presented in col.10 was 0.44. The standard error of multiple estimate indicates that achievement would increase by 12.44 units (col.7) for every unit increase in attitude. The constant value that would be considered in the equation at the end of first step with which the prediction of achievement in writing would be possible is as shown in col.9. The general form of the prediction equation may be given as:

$$x^1 = a + b_1 x_1 + b_2 x_2 + b_3 x_3 + \dots\dots\dots + b_n x_n$$

Where x^1 denotes the predicted score of the dependent variable, A is the constant, b_1, b_2, b_3 .... bn partial regression co-efficient and x_1, x_2, x_3.........xn are obtained values on different independent variables. Thus, the actual equation at the end of the first step would be.

Writing achievement = 15.17 + 14.12 (Attitude) ... *(1.1)*

The second variable that entered into the stepwise regression analysis was age. The multiple correlation obtained between writing achievement and the two independent variables namely attitude and age was 0.49 per cent (col.3). Thus, the strength of the relationship between writing achievement and the two independent variables put together was 0.49 per cent. The relationship was significant at 0.01 level as the 'F' value 57.03 was far beyond the table value for 2 and 357 degrees of freedom. The two variables put together could explain about 24 per cent (R^2 = 0.24) of the variance in the dependent variable i.e., writing achievement. The partial regression co-efficient shown in col.7 disclosed that when attitude and age were included as predictor variables achievement of neo-literates in writing would increase by 8.44 and 7.78 points for every unit of increase in attitude and age respectively. Both the partial regression co-efficiently ('t' values) were significant at 0.01 level as shown in col.8. The regression equation to predict achievement in writing with attitude and age as predictor variables was

Writing achievement = 17.11 + 8.44 (attitude) + 7.78 (age) .... *(1.2)*

In the hierarchy of predictor variables associated with writing achievement of neo-literates Factor A entered as the next important variable. The multiple correlation of the combined association of attitude, age and Factor A was 0.52 (col.3) which was significant at 0.01 level (F' = 45.57 for 3 and 356 degrees of freedom). The value of R^2 (0.27) (col.4) disclosed that about 27 per cent of variance in writing achievement was explained by these three variables. Out of this variance 18.57 per cent was explained by attitude, 2.98 per cent by age and 6.19 per cent by Factor A. When the three predictor variable were considered the partial regression co-efficient (col.7) indicted that the increase in writing achievement was 6.66, 4.37 and 4.95 units for every unit increase in attitude, age and Factor A. The three 't' values obtained were significant at 0.01 level. The regression equation at this step with constant 19.50 was

Writing achievement = 19.50 + 6.66 (attitude) + 4.37 (age) 4.95 (Factor A) ... *(1.3)*

The next variable that entered into the step wise regression analysis was 'Factor B'. The multiple R was 0.57. The 'F' value obtained (43.41 for 4 and 355 degrees of freedom) was significant beyond 0.01 level. The value of R^2 (0.32) revealed that the combined strength of relationship between attitude, age, Factor A and Factor B and the dependent variable writing achievement was 32 per cent. The contribution of each of the predictor variables was 17.87 attitude, 2.26 age, 8.06 Factor A and 4.64 'Factor B'. The standard error of multiple estimate indicated that 68 per cent of the obtained writing achievement scores would be without the range of ± 8.74 points (col.5) units of predicted scores of achievement. The partial regression co-efficients (col.7) disclosed that when the four variable namely, attitude, age, Factor A and Factor B were included in the regression analysis, the writing achievement would increased by 8.76, 4.29, 3.40, 3.06 points for every unit increase in the above variables respectively. The regression co-efficient which would predict writing achievement was

Writing achievement = *24.54 + 8.76 (attitude) + 4.29 (age) + 3.40 (Factor A) + 3.06 (Factor B)* ... *(1.4)*

The next variable that entered into the regression analysis was 'caste'. The multiple correlation obtained between writing achievement and the independent variables namely, attitude, age, factor A, factor B and caste was 0.59. The relationship was significant at 0.01 level as the 'F' value of 39.58 for 5 and 354 degrees of freedom was far beyond the table value. The five variables put together explained about 35 per cent of the variance in the writing achievement of neo-literates. The standard error of multiple estimate revealed that about 68 per cent of the obtained achievement scores would be within the range of 6.95 units of predicted achievement scores. The regression equation with the constant 28.99 was

Writing achievement = *28.99 + 8.74 (Attitude) + 7.78 (age) + 5.41 (Factor A) + 3.12 (Factor B) + 4.57 (caste)* ... *(1.5)*

The next variable that entered into the regression analysis was 'Factor Q_1'. The multiple correlation obtained between writing achievement and the six independent variables namely, attitude, age, factor A, factor B, caste and Factor Q_1, was 0.61 per cent (col.3). The strength of the relationship between writing achievement and the six independent variables put together was (0.61 per cent). The relationship was significant at 0.01 level as the F value of 36.49 was far beyond the table value for 6 and 353 degrees of freedom. The six variables put together could explain about 38 per cent of variance in the dependent variable i.e., writing achievement. The standard error of multiple estimate SE of R shown in col.5 revealed that nearly 68 per cent of the writing achievement scores would be within the range of ± 5.21 points of predicted writing achievement scores. The partial regression co-efficient shown in col.7 indicated that when the six independent variables namely, attitude, age, Factor A, Factor B, caste and Factor Q_1 were included as predictor variables achievement of neo-literates in writing would increase by 8.54, 6.71, 5.59, 3.46, 1.48 and 2.07 points respectively. All the partial regression co-efficiently (t′ values) were significant at 0.01 level as shown in col.8. The regression equation to predict achievement in writing at this step was

Writing achievement = *33.15 + 8.54 (Attitude) + 6.71 (age) + 5.59 (Factor A) + 3.46 (Factor B) + 1.48 (Caste) + 2.07 (Factor* Q_1*)* ...*(1.6)*

These out of the 23 independent variables namely, gender, age, caste, occupation, marital status, income, Factor A, Factor B, Factor C, Factor E, Factor F, Factor G, Factor H, Factor I, Factor L, Factor M, Factor N, Factor O, Factor Q_1, Factor Q_2, Factor Q_3, Factor Q_4, attitude only 6 variables namely have significantly predicted the writing achievement of neo-literates. Thus, in brief, the variance explained by the six variables was given in the table on next page.

Hence, the null hypothesis that ‘No single variable or a set of variables included in the study do not significantly exert their contribution to writing achievement of neo-literates’ is rejected except in case of variables viz., attitude, age, Factor A, Factor B, Caste and Factor Q_1

Sl. No.	Independent Variable	Percentage of variance explained
1	Attitude	16.85
2	Age	3.01
3	Factor A	8.53
4	Factor B	5.25
5	Caste	1.97
6	Factor Q_1	2.65
	Total	**38.26**

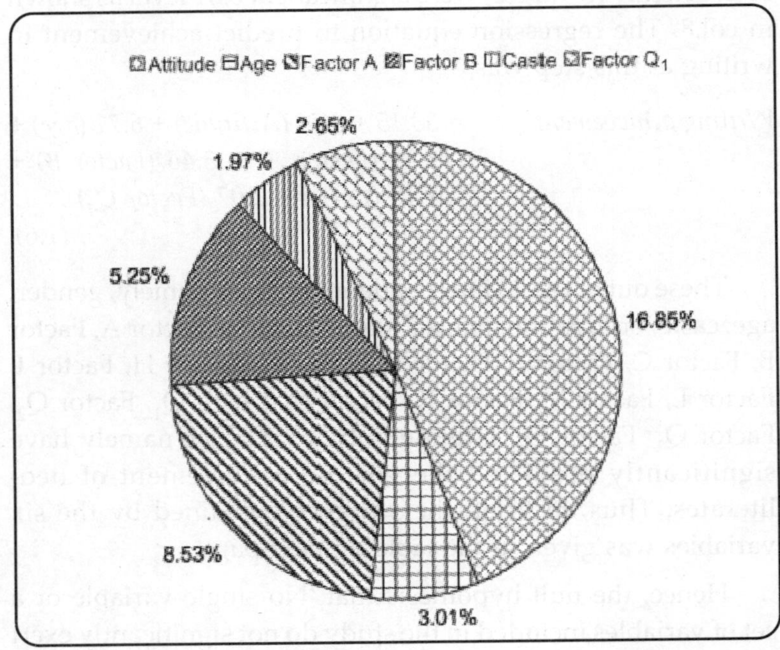

Fig. 5.11 : Percentage of Variance Explained by Independent Variables on Writing Achievement

Factors Predicting Achievement of Neo-literates in Numeracy

Detailed analysis of the step-wise regression analysis on achievement of neo-literates in numeracy is shown in Table 5.36. Out of 23 independent variables considered for analysis i.e., gender, age, caste, occupation, marital status, income, Factor A, Factor B, Factor C, Factor E, Factor F, Factor G, Factor H, Factor I, Factor L, Factor M, Factor N, Factor O, Factor Q_1, Factor Q_2, Factor Q_3, Factor Q_4, attitude only 5 variables were significantly related and explained 35 per cent of variance in the numeracy achievement of neo-literates. It may be seen from the table that the first variable that entered into the stepwise multiple regression analysis is Factor B. The multiple correlation R (col.3) 0.41 which is nothing but simple correlation shown in col. 11 between the dependent variable achievement in numeracy' and the most influencing variable 'Factor B'. The value indicated that the strength of the relationship between the two as 11.10 (vide col.7). It may be observed that 'R' was significant at 0.01 level (74.96 for 1 and 358 degrees of freedom) (vide col.6). The standard error of multiple estimate (col.5) (10.55) revealed that nearly 68 per cent of the obtained achievement scores were within the range of ± 10.55 point of predicted numeracy achievement scores. The partial regression co-efficient or β co-efficient presented in col.7 was 11.10. This value indicates that achievement would increase by 11.10 units (col.7) for every unit increase in Factor B. The constant value that would be considered in the equation at the end of the first step with which the prediction of achievement in numeracy would be possible is as shown in col.9. Thus, the actual equation at the end of the first step would be:

Numeracy achievement = *17.85 + 11.10 (Factor B)* ... *(1.1)*

The second variable that entered into the stepwise regression analysis was 'attitude'. The multiple correlation obtained between numercy achievement and the two independent variables namely, Factor B and attitude 0.48 per

Table 5.36 : Factors significantly influencing Neo-literates achievement in Numeracy as denoted by proportion of variance explained (R^2) by multiple Regression Analysis

Step No.	Independent variable entered in each step	Multiple correlation R	R^2	Standard error of multiple estimate	F-value (d.f) and level of significance	B-co-efficient or B-partial regression co-efficient	t-value for B and level of significance	Constant	B-Beta co-efficient	Simple correlation co-efficient with dependent	Percentage of variance explained by each independent variable
1	Factor B	0.41	0.17	10.55	74.96 (1,358)	11.10	9.22	17.85	0.52	0.41	0.21
2	Attitude	0.48	0.23	12.47	62.77 (2,357)	8.08 8.36	1.91 5.22	18.62	0.18 0.40	0.38	0.19 0.40
3	Factor H	0.55	0.31	16.67	46.77 (3,356)	8.01 7.72 6.25	4.90 5.41 4.90	22.63	0.45 0.57 0.36	0.26	0.17 0.08 0.06
4	Marital status	0.58	0.33	12.31	40.89 (3,554)	6.84 5.45 3.90 2.04	1.76 3.05 5.46 2.92	32.63	0.63 0.83 0.78 0.56	0.24	0.15 0.07 0.05 0.03
5	Income	0.59	0.35	15.08	49.64 (5,354)	5.74 3.82 6.76 4.33 2.79	3.71 5.86 4.48 2.95 2.00	38.77	0.55 0.62 0.59 0.45 0.31	0.18	0.10 0.09 0.07 0.03 0.06

cent (col.3). Thus, the strength of the relationship between achievement in numeracy and the two independent variables put together was 48 per cent. The relationship was significant at 0.01 level as the 'F' value 62.77 was far beyond the table value for 2 and 357 degrees of freedom. The two variables put together could explain about 23 per cent ($R^2 = 0.23$) of the variance in the dependent variable i.e., numeracy achievement. The standard error of multiple estimate (SE of R) in col.5 revealed that nearly 68 per cent of the obtained numeracy achievement scores would be within the range of ± 12.47 (col.5) points of predicted numeracy achievement. The partial regression co-efficient shown in col.7 disclosed that when Factor B and attitude were included as predictor variables achievement of neo-literates in numeracy would increase by 8.08 and 8.36 points for every unit of increase in Factor B and attitude respectively. Both the partial regression co-efficient ('t' values) were significant at 0.01 level as shown in col.8. The regression equation to predict achievement in numeracy with Factor B and attitude as predictor variables was

Numeracy achievement = *18.62 + 8.08 (Factor B) + 8.36 (Attitude)* ... *(1.2)*

In the hierarchy of predictor variables associated with numeracy achievement of learners 'Factor H' entered as the next important variable. The multiple correlation of the combined association of Factor B, attitude and Factor H was 0.55 (col.3) which was significant at 0.01 level ('F' = 46.77 for 3 and 356 degrees of freedom). The value of R2 (0.31) (col.4) disclosed that about 31 per cent of variance in numeracy achievement was explained by these three variables. Out of this variance 17 per cent was explained by Factor B, 8 per cent by attitude and 6 per cent by Factor H. When the three predictor variables were considered the partial regression co-efficient (col.7) indicated that the increase in numeracy achievement was 8.01, 7.72 and 6.25 units for every unit increase in Factor B, attitude and Factor H. The three 't' values obtained were significant at 0.01 level. The regression equation at this step with constant 22.63 was

Numeracy achievement = 22.63 + 8.01 (*Factor B*) + 7.72 (*Attitude*) + 6.25 (*Factor H*) ....(*1.3*)

The next variable that entered in to the step wise regression analysis was 'marital status'. The multiple R was 0.58. The 'F' value obtained 40.89 for 4 and 354 degrees of freedom) was significant beyond 0.01 level. The value of R^2 (0.33) revealed that the combined strength of relationship between Factor B, attitude, Factor H, and marital status and the dependent variable numeracy achievement was 33 per cent. The contribution of each of the predictor variables was 15.00 per cent Factor B, 7.00 percent attitude, 5.00 percent Factor H and 3.00 per cent marital status. The standard error of multiple estimate indicated that 68 per cent of the obtained numeracy achievement scores would be without the range of ± 12.31 points (col.5) units of predicted scores of achievement in numeracy. The partial regression co-efficients (col.7) disclosed that when the four variables namely, Factor B, attitude, Factor H marital status were included in the regression analysis, the numeracy achievement would increase by 6.84, 5.45, 3.90 and 2.04 units for every unit increase in the 4 variables respectively. The regression equation which would predict numeracy achievement was

Numeracy achievement = 32.63 + 6.84 (*Factor B* + 5.45 (*Attitude*) + 3.90 (*factor H*) + 2.04 (*Marital status*) ...(*1.4*)

The next variable that entered the regression analysis was 'income'. The obtained multiple R was 0.59. The F value 49.64 was significant beyond 0.01 level for 5 and 354 degrees of freedom. The co-efficient of multiple regression (R^2) revealed that the combined strength of relationship between the independent variables i.e., Factor B, attitude, Factor H, marital status and income and the dependent variable achievement in numeracy was 35 per cent. The standard error of multiple estimate revealed that 68 per cent of the obtained numercy achievement scores would be within the range of ± 15.08 (col.5) points of predicted scores of numeracy achievement. The partial regression co-efficient (col.7) revealed that when the 5 independent values namely, Factor B, attitude, Factor H, marital status and income were included in the regression analysis, the achievement in numeracy would increase by 5.74, 3.82, 6.76, 4.33 and 2.79 for every unit increase in the 5 variables respectively. The regression equation as this step would be

Numeracy achievement = *38.77+5.74 (Factor B) + 3.82 (Attitude) + 6.76 (Factor H) + 4.33 (marital status) + 2.79 (income)* ... *(1.5)*

Thus, out of 23 independent variables namely gender, age, caste, occupation, marital status, income, Factor A, Factor B, Factor C, Factor E, Factor F, Factor G, Factor H, Factor I, Factor L, Factor M, Factor N, Factor O, Factor Q_1, Factor Q_2, Factor Q_3, Factor Q_4, attitude significantly predicted the achievement of neo-literates in numeracy. Thus, in brief, the variance explained by the 5 variables was as follows:

Sl.No.	Independent Variable	Percentage of variance explained
1.	Factor B	10.00
2	Attitude	9.00
3	Factor H	7.00
4	Marital status	3.00
5	Income	6.00
	Total	**35.00**

Hence, the null hypothesis that 'no single variable or a set of variables included in the study do not significantly exert their contribution to numeracy achievement of neo-literates is rejected except in case of variables viz., Factor B, attitude, Factor H, marital status and income.

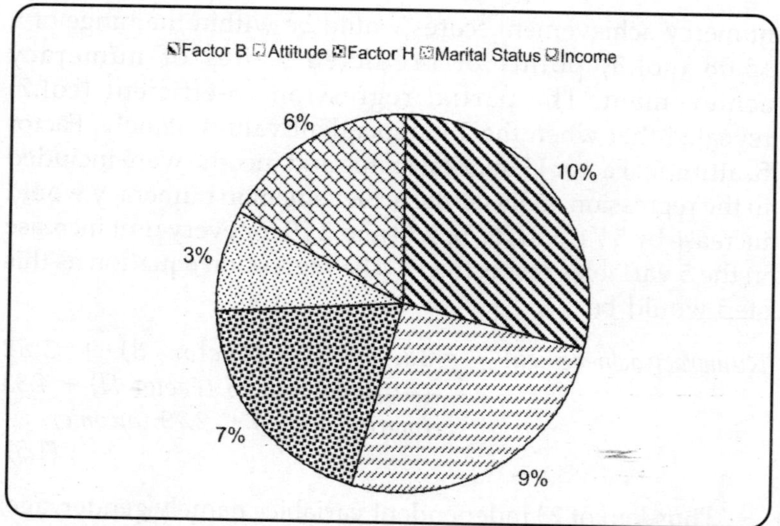

Fig. 5.12 : Percentage of Variance Explained by Independent Vairables on Numeracy Achievement

Factors Predicting Total Achievement of Neo-literates

Detailed analysis of the step-wise regression analysis on total achievement of neo-literates is presented in table 37. Out of 23 independent variables considered for analysis i.e., gender, age, caste, occupation, marital status, income, Factor A, Factor B, Factor C, Factor E, Factor F, Factor G, Factor H, Factor I, Factor L, Factor M, Factor N, Factor O, Factor Q_1, Factor Q_2, Factor Q_3, Factor Q_4, only 6 attitude variables were significantly related and explained 47 per cent of variance in the total achievement of neo-literates.. It may be seen from the table that the first variable that entered into the stepwise multiple regression analysis is attitude. The multiple correlation R (col.3) is 0.55. The value indicated that the strength of the relationship between the two variables i.e., attitude and total achievement as 18.67 (vid col.7). It may be observed that 'R' was significant at 0.01 level 159.66 for 1 and 358 degrees of freedom) (vide col.6). The co-efficient of multiple determination R_2 disclosed that about 30.00 per cent

Table 5.37 : Factors significantly influencing Neo-literates in Total Achievement as denoted by proportion of variance explained (R^2) by multiple Regression Analysis.

Step No.	Independent variable entered in each step	Multiple correlation R	R^2	Standard error of multiple estimate	F-value (d.f) and level of signifi-cance	B-co-efficient or B-partial regression co-efficient	t-value for B and level of signifi-cance	Constant	B-Beta co-efficient	Simple correla-tion co-efficient with depen-dent	Percentage of variance explained by each indepen-dent variable
1	2	3	4	5	6	7	8	9	10	11	12
1	Attitude	0.55	0.30	13.02	159.66 (1,358)	18.67	12.64	66.70	-0.55	0.55	30.84
2	Factor B	0.60	0.36	16.64	102.63 (2,357)	17.77 8.29	11.67 5.64	78.22	-0.24 -0.49	0.50	27.63 8.67
3	Income	0.63	0.39	11.79	78.38 (3,356)	17.69 8.37 7.40	11.63 5.86 4.40	85.11	-0.49 -0.24 -0.18	0.39	27.34 8.98 3.45
4	Age	0.66	0.43	11.03	68.83 (4,355)	17.74 9.47 7.02 6.74	12.09 7.02 5.25 4.96	91.00	-0.49 -0.29 -0.21 -0.20	0.33	27.52 10.70 4.03 1.42

1	2	3	4	5	6	7	8	9	10	11	12
5	Marital Status	0.67	0.45	10.68	59.21 (5,354)	17.88 9.71 6.97 5.73 2.86	12.47 6.93 5.29 4.21 3.48	96.88	-0.50 -0.28 -0.21 -0.17 -0.14	0.28	28.02 10.42 4.01 1.21 1.88
6	Factor Q_1	0.68	0.47	9.44	53.00 (6,353)	15.68 8.69 6.24 5.14 3.41 4.96	10.24 6.17 4.75 3.80 4.14 3.52	100.67	-0.35 -0.25 -0.18 -0.15 -0.16 -0.21	0.24	26.92 9.32 3.58 1.05 2.24 4.24

of variance (vide col.3) in the total achievement was accounted by attitude. The standard error of multiple estimate (col.5) revealed that nearly 68 per cent of the obtained achievement scores were within the range of ± 13.02 points of predicted total achievement scores. The constant value that would be considered in the equation at the end of the first step with which the prediction of total achievement would be possible is as shown in col.9. The actual equation at the end of the first step would be:

Total achievement = 66.70 + 18.67 (Attitude). . *(1.1)*

The second variable that entered into the stepwise regression analysis was factor B. The multiple correlation obtained between total achievement and the two independent variables namely, attitude and factor B was 0.60 (col.3). Thus, the strength of the relationship between total achievement and the two independent variables put together was 60 per cent. The relationship was significant at 0.01 level as the 'F' value 102.63 was far beyond the table value for 2 and 357 degrees of freedom. The two variables put together could explain about 36 per cent (R_2 = 0.36) of the variance in the dependent variable i.e., total achievement. The standard error of multiple estimate (SE of R) in col.5 revealed that nearly 68 per cent of the obtained total achievement scores would be with in the range of ± 6.64 (col.5) points of predicted total achievement. The partial regression co-efficient shown in col.7 disclosed that when attitude and factor B were included as predictor variables total achievement of neo-literates would increase by 17.77 and 8.29 points for every unit of increase in attitude and factor B respectively. Both the partial regression co-efficients ('t' values) were significant at 0.01 level as shown in col.8. The regression equation to predict total achievement with attitude and factor B as predictor variables was

Total achievement = *78.22 + 17.77 (attitude) + 8.29 (Factor B)* *(1.2)*

In the hierarchy of predictor variables associated with total achievement of learners 'income' entered as the next important variable. The multiple correlation of the combined association of attitude, factor B, and income was 0.63 (col.3) which was significant at 0.01 level ('F' = 78.38 for 3 and 356 degrees of freedom). The value of R2 (0.39) (col.4) disclosed that about 39 per cent of variance in total achievement was explained by these three variables. Out of this variance 27.34 per cent was explained by attitude 8.98 per cent by Factor B and 3.45 per cent by income. When the three predictor variables were considered the partial regression co-efficients (col.7) indicated that the increase in total achievement was 17.69, 8.37 and 7.40 units for every unit increase in attitude, factor B and income. The three 't' values obtained were significant at 0.01 level. The regression equation at this step with constant 85.11 was

Total achievement = *85.11 + 17.69 (Attitude) + 8.37 (Factor B) + 7.4 (income)* ...(1.3)

The next variable that entered into the step wise regression analysis was age. The multiple R was 0.66. The 'F' value obtained 68.83 for 4 and 355 degrees of freedom) was significant beyond 0.01 level. The value of R^2 (0.43) revealed that the combined strength of relationship between the four independent variables and the dependent variable total achievement was 43 per cent. The contribution of each of the predictor variables was 27.52 attitude, 10.70 factor B, 4.03 income and 1.42 age. The standard error of multiple estimate indicated that 68 per cent of the obtained total achievement scores would be without the range of ±11.03 points (col.5) predicted scores of achievement. The partial regression co-efficient (col.7) disclosed that when the four variables namely, attitude, factor B, income and age were included in the regression analysis, the total achievement would increase by 17.74, 9.47, 7.02 and 6.74 units for every unit increase in the 4 variables respectively. The regression co-efficient which would predict total achievement was

Total achievement = *91.00 + 17.74 (Attitude) + 9.47 (factor B) + 7.02 (Income) + 6.74 (age)* ... (1.4)

The next variable that entered into the regression analysis was 'marital status'. The multiple correlation obtained between total achievement and the independent variables namely, attitude, factor B, income, age and marital status was 0.67. The relationship was significant at 0.01 level as the 'F' value of 59.21 for 5 and 354 degrees of freedom) was far beyond the table value. The five variables put together explained about 45 per cent of the variance in the total achievement of neo-literates. The standard error of multiple estimate revealed that 68 per cent of the obtained achievement scores would be within the range of ± 10.68 units of predicted total achievement scores. The regression equation with the constant 96.88 was

Total achievement = *96.88 + 17.88 (Attitude) + 9.71 (Factor B) + 6.97 (Income) + 5.73 (age) + 2.86 (Marital status)* ... *(1.5)*

Factor Q_1 of 16 PF entered as the sixth variable in the regression analysis. The multiple R 0.68 was significant beyond 0.01 level for 6 and 353 degrees of freedom. The six dependent variables put together explained 47 per cent of the variance in the total achievement of adult learners. Out of this 26.92, 9.32, 3.58, 1.05, 2.24 and 4.24 per cent of variance was explained by the variables—attitude, factor B, income, age, marital status and factor Q_1. The standard error of multiple estimate (SE of R) reveled that nearly 68 per cent of the obtained total achievement scores would be with the range of ± 9.44 units of predicted total achievement scores. The regression equation with constant 100.67 was

Total achievement = *100.67 + 15.68 (Attitude) + 8.69 (Factor B) + 6.24 (Income) + 5.14 (age) + 3.41 (Marital status) + 4.96 (Factor* Q_1*)* ... *(1.6)*

Hence, out of 23 independent variables gender, age, caste, occupation, marital status, income, Factor A, Factor B, Factor

C, Factor E, Factor F, Factor G, Factor H, Factor I, Factor L, Factor M, Factor N, Factor O, Factor Q_1, Factor Q_2, Factor Q_3, Factor Q_4, attitude only 6 variables predicted the total achievement of neo-literates. Thus, in brief, the variance explained by the six variables was as follows:

Sl. No.	Independent Variable	Percentage of variance explained
1	Attitude	26.92
2	Factor B	9.32
3	Income	3.58
4	Age	1.05
5	Marital status	2.24
6	Factor Q_1	4.24
	Total	**47.35**

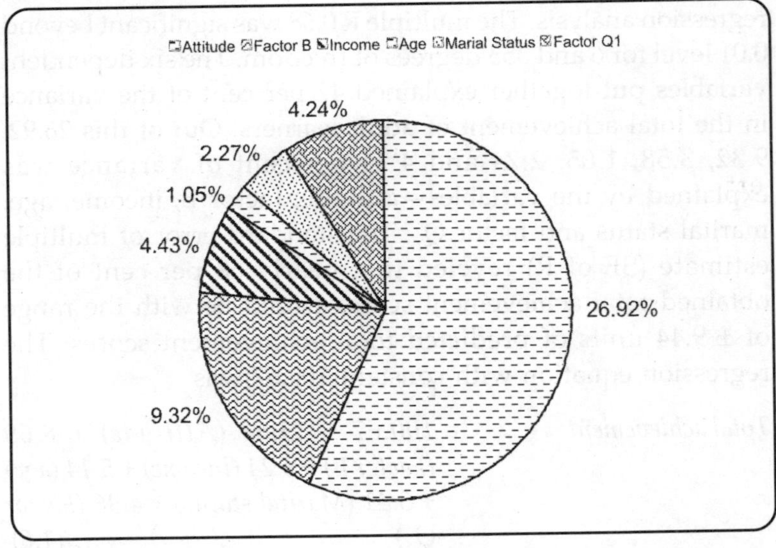

Fig. 5.13 : Percentage of Variance Explained by Independent Variables on Total Achievement

Hence the null hypothesis that 'No single variable or a set of variables include in the study do not significantly exert their contribution to total performance of neo-literates rejected with respect to 6 variables namely, attitude, factor B, income age, martial status and factor Q_1. The summary, conclusions and suggestions for further research are presented in the next chapter.

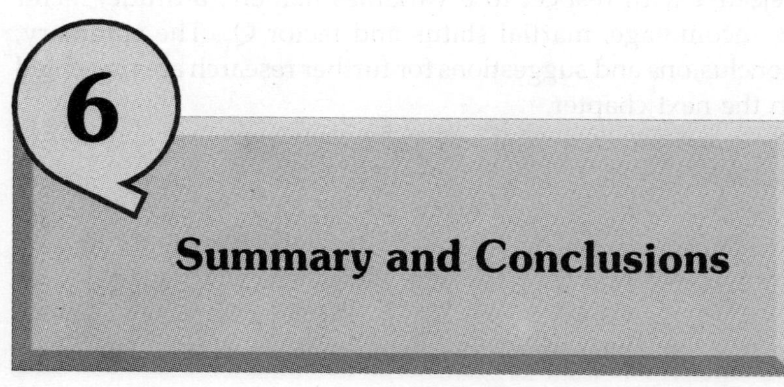

6 Summary and Conclusions

Introduction

The vital relationship between education and national development needs hardly to be over-emphasized. Education has all along been a powerful instrument of social, economic, political and cultural change and it thereby gave strong impetus to national development. In the ultimate process of development, the role of education is to impart knowledge, understanding, attitudes and skills to human resources and in turn make these resources qualified to utilize the physical resources fully and effectively. The contribution of education to national development is being increasingly realized today more than ever before and development is now conceived primarily as a process of education and human resource development.

India cannot achieve economic development, social transformation and effective social security until and unless the citizens are educated to the extent that enables them to participate in the country's developmental programmes, willingly, intelligently and effectively. Illiteracy as a mass phenomenon blocks economic and social progress, affects health and community hygiene, population control, national integration and security. Illiterate people tend to resist change and cling to traditionalistic forms of life. New ideas and new practices cannot be effectively communicated to those who are untrained to receive them and make use of them. Therefore, there is a need to reshape and change the attitude of masses through education and training. Adult Education emphasizes upon three main components namely, literacy, functionality and awareness. Literacy which is supposed to be a stepping stone for education includes the three rudimentary skills of reading, writing and numeracy and is considered as a minimum need for every human being to have a better life in the society. Functional literacy implies self-reliance in literacy and numeracy, becoming aware of the causes for their deprivation and moving towards amelioration of their conditions through organization and participation in the process of development, acquiring skills to improve the economic status and general well-being, imbibing the values of national integration, conservation of the environment, women's equality, observance of small family norms, etc. Functionality more or less is concerned with making the individual to function well individually, socially, culturally and economically. Adult education in India does not end with providing literacy, functionality and awareness. It extends further leading to life long education and continuing education. The scope of adult education extends to all sections of the community and it is a pre-condition to accelerate the pace and magnitude of development.

Recognising the need for the education of masses, India has implemented several literacy programmes especially after independence (Social Education Programme, 1949; Community Development Programme, 1951; Farmers' Functional Literacy Programme, 1966-67; Non-formal Education Programmes, 1975; National Adult Education Programme, 1978; Point No.16 of the New 20 Point

Programme, 1982; Mass Programme for Functional Literacy, 1986; National Literacy Mission, 1988) and Total Literacy Campaigns, 1989-90 onwards. The scheme of continuing education was introduced from 1995 onwards through the establishment of continuing education centres. Neo –literates are the main beneficiaries of continuing education programme. The literacy rate of the country has increased from 16.67 in 1951 to 65.38 during 2001. As per part of the National Literacy Mission, the Government of Andhra Pradesh has implemented total literacy campaigns, post-literacy and continuing education programmes, Akshara Sankranthi (2001-04), and Akshara Bharati Programmes (2 phases) (2005-06 and 2006-07). A good number of neo-literates are participating in the continuing education centres and it is necessary to know the level of proficiency they have achieved in literacy skills, and the associated factors.

Statement of the Problem

"A Study on the Performance of Neo-literates in Relation to Certain Socio-Psychological Factors in Chittoor District".

Need for the Study

Attainment in literacy skills refers to proficiency in 3 R's or reading, writing and in numeracy skills. The total score obtained by the learner on all the three components of literacy can be stated as total achievement. How an individual has achieved proficiency in basic literacy skills depends upon how effectively he learns. Existing research studies in the field of adult education indicate that several socio-psychological factors and environmental factors operate and influence the learning behaviour, which ultimately decide the level of achievement of literacy skills by an individual.

Some research studies vide chapter II indicate that women achieve better than men and certain other studies indicate that men are better than women. Yet there are studies which denote that gender has no impact on the achievement. On the whole, there appears the need to explore the impact of gender on the achievement of neo-literates who are attending the continuing education centres. Age is yet another important variable which deserves attention. Some research studies (vide chapter II) have shown that the lower age group have performed better in achieving literacy skills where some others have found that high age group have performed better an literacy skills. Further, there are studies which have revealed that age has no impact on the achievement of neo-literates. Hence there is need to explore the impact of age on the performance of neo-literates attending the continuing education centres. With age comes growth and with growth, an individual's fund of experience involving a wide variety of situations increases steadily. Experience helps an individual to modify his behaviour and method of dealing with situations so that he may be more efficient. Hence, age in as much as it reflects the degree of maturity and experience may affect the achievement of an individual.

In India people representing Scheduled Castes and Scheduled Tribes are deprived of certain economic and social benefits as a result of which some of these people may lack confidence regarding their own abilities and capacities. This may lead to variation in the achievement between learners representing Scheduled Castes and Scheduled Tribes versus other castes. Hence, there appears the need to know the impact of caste on achievement of learners.

In addition to the above, personality is another variable that has potential influence on learners achievement of literacy skills. Personality characteristics like introversion, extroversion, emotional maturity, flexibility, anxiety, imaginativeness, boldness, conservatism, fatalism, cheerfulness, and the like influence the behaviour of a person in carrying out a task. It is likely that neo-literates with different levels of their personality characteristics may differ in the manner in which they go about in achieving literacy skills. Therefore, it would be of interest to examine how personality factors are related to the achievement of the learners.

Attitude has a major role to play in enabling the learners to participate in the literacy centres. In operational terms, attitude refers to the details of what people think or feel on the way in which they intend to act. It may be generally around that attitude of a learner towards various aspects of adult education programme like benefits, community support, instruction, supervision, type of present literacy activities enhances his level of achievements. Some of the studies as presented in chapter II have revealed that attitude influences the performance of adult learners/neo-literates and such studies are quite limited. Hence there is need for empirical investigations relating to the impact of attitude on the performance of neo-literates.

In the light of the forgoing considerations, it may be assumed that differences in personal factors (gender, age), social factors (caste, marital status), economic factors (occupation, income), and personality factors (16 PF and attitude) may significantly influence the performance of neo-literates, attending the continuing education centres.

The Government of India and non-government organisations are making a lot effort to eradicate of illiteracy in our country. The effective implementation of total literacy campaigns has contributed towards the substantial increase of neo-literates and semi-literates. But due to lack of immediate post-literacy activities at the grassroot level and due to lack of people's participation in the continuing education centres the neo-literates and semi-literates are again relapsing into illiteracy. The non-enrolment and dropout at primary level and at adult education centres, poor socio-economic conditions are other reasons is leading to the problem of illiteracy in the country. How to check the problem? What types of efforts are basically required to promote adult education in the country? Illiteracy is a global problem. Studies that deal with the basic aspects of learning or achievement in relation to different personal, social, economic and programme related factors would of immense help to the programme planners and executives to design effective strategies. The present study which is related to the on-going programme of adult education would be of greater help to the district administrations to chalk out effective strategies for promoting the literacy, post-literacy and continuing education programmes.

Objectives of the Study

1. To study the influence of personal, social and economic factors (gender, age, caste, marital status, occupation and income) on the achievement of neo-literates;
2. To know the influence of personality factors (as measured by Cattell's 16 PF)on the achievement of neo-literates;
3. To estimate the impact of attitude of neo-literates on their achievement;
4. To understand the contribution of different variables to achievement of neo-literates in literacy skills.

Hypotheses

Based on the above objectives, the following hypotheses were formulated for testing. Each variable has been tested separately.

1. Gender does not significantly influence the achievement of neo-literates in literacy skills and total achievement.
2. Age does not significantly influence the achievement of neo-literates in literacy skills and total achievement.
3. Caste does not significantly influence the achievement of neo-literates in literacy skills and total achievement.

4. Occupation does not significantly influence the achievement of neo-literates in literacy skills and total achievement.
5. Marital status does not significantly influence the achievement of neo-literates in literacy skills and total achievement.
6. Income does not significantly influence the achievement of neo-literates in literacy skills and total achievement.
7. Personality factors (as measured by Cattell's 16 PF) do not significantly influence the achievement of neo-literates in literacy skills and total achievement.
8. Attitude towards adult education does not significantly influence the achievement of neo-literates in literacy skills and total achievement.
9. No single variable or a set of variables included in the study do not significantly exert their contribution to the reading achievement of neo-literates.
10. No single variable or a set of variables included in the study do not significantly exert their contribution to the writing achievement of neo-literates.
11. No single variable or a set of variables included in the study do not significantly exert their contribution to the numeracy achievement of neo-literates.
12. No single variable or a set of variables included in the study do not significantly exert their contribution to the total achievement of neo-literates.

Variables Studied

Dependent Variables

The dependent variables are Achievement in: (1) Achievement in Reading; (2) Achievement in Writing; (3) Achievement in Numeracy; and (4) Total Achievement which is the total score on reading, writing and numeracy.

Independent Variables

The independent variables included in the study are: (1) Gender (male, female); (2) Age (15-25 years, 25-35 years, 36 years and above); (3) Caste (Scheduled Castes, Scheduled Tribes, Backward Caste and Others); (4) Occupation (agriculture, non-agriculture), (5)Marital status (married and unmarried); (6) Income (Below Rs.10,000/- per year and Rs.10,000 and above per year); (7) 16 Personality factors(as measured by Cattell's 16 PF Form-E) and (8)Attitude towards adult education.

Tools Developed

For the purpose of the present study to following tools were developed by the investigator:

1. Achievement test for measuring the level of proficiency in reading, writing, and numeracy skills;
2. Attitude scale towards adult education;
3. The Personality Factor Questionnaire (Cattell's 16 PF – Form E) was adopted for the present study.

Personal data sheet was used to know the socio-economic aspects of the neo-literates learners.

Selection of the Sample

Chittoor district consists of 66 mandals continuing education centres are organized in all the mandals. Multi-stage random sampling method was used for selecting the sample. At the first stage 6 mandals were randomly selected. Each mandal consists of 15-25 continuing education centres. At the second stage, 5 continuing education centres were randomly selected. From each of the continuing education centres at the third stage a sample of 12 neo-literates were randomly selected. Thus the sample of the study was 360 neo-literates (6 x 5 x 12 = 360 learners)

The lists of the centres and preraks organizing continuing education centres were collected from the office of the Zilla Saksharatha Samathi, Chittoor. The list of neo-literates were collected from the prerak, volunteers in order to select the learners by adopting simple random sampling.

Collection of Data

The data required for the study was collected from the learners by contacting them individually at the centres. Necessary rapport was established before collecting the data from them. The help of the Prerak was sought by the investigator in administering the tools. The measures were administered to the learners in 2 sessions. In the first session, achievement test was administered. During the second session, measure of attitude, and 16 PF questionnaire were administered. An interval of 15-30 minutes was given between the administration of the tests. It took approximately two hours for the completion of all the tools by each neo-literate. Personal data relating to the learner's name, gender, age, caste, occupation, marital status and income was collected by utilizing the personal data sheet. Thus the final data relating to study was collected.

Analysis of Data

The data collected was analysed by using relevant statistical techniques like 't' test and 'F' test to find out the differences among the groups. The multiple correlation 'R' was calculated by carrying out stepwise regression analysis.

Findings of the Study

The major findings of the study are as follows:

1. The sample of the study consisted of 360 neo-literates attending the continuing education centres in Chittoor district. They have received literacy instruction from the preraks. The neo-literates of the

sample have received certificate and all of them are enrolled in the continuing education centres.

2. The variable wise distribution of the sample revealed that majority were represented by women sample (55.00 percent) and the remaining 45.00 per cent were represented by men group.
3. 43.05 per cent of the sample belonged to 15-25 years and 25.00 per cent belonged to 26-35 years and the remaining 31.95 belonged to 36 years and above age group. National Literacy Mission gives priority to 15-35 years age group and more than two thirds of the sample are represented by this age group.
4. Caste-wise details of the sample revealed that 47.22 percent belonged to forward castes, 33.61 per cent belonged to backward castes and the remaining 19.17 per cent belonged to scheduled castes and scheduled tribes.
5. Two thirds of the sample (66.67 per cent) are represented by married group and the remaining one third (33.33 per cent) are represented by unmarried group.
6. More than half of the sample (53.61 per cent) belonged to agricultural group and the remaining 46.39 per cent belonged to non-agricultural group (tailoring, brick making, business activities etc.).
7. More than half of the sample (54.44 per cent are represented by lower income group (below Rs.10,000/- per year) and the remaining 45.56 per cent of the sample are represented by higher Income group (Rs.10,000/- and above per year)
8. Literacy test was administered to the sample of neo-literates. The results showed that 63.33 per cent of the sample have achieved the literacy level as per norms.

9. The achievement scores of learners are normally distributed. The reading test is for 40 marks, writing test is for 30 marks and the numeracy test is for 30 marks. The mean, median and mode of the reading scores test are 26.54, 26.77 and 27.23 respectively. Similarly, the mean, median and mode of the writing test scores are 18.55, 18.08 and 17.54. For numeracy test, the scores are 17.95, 17.80 and 17.50. In case of total achievement scores, the mean, median and mode are 63.08, 64.17 and 66.35. The scores of neo-literates on reading test are better followed by writing and numeracy tests.
10. Gender has significantly influenced the achievement of neo-literates with respect to reading, writing, numeracy and total achievement. The mean differences indicated better achievement of women group in relation to their counterparts in all the sub-tests and total achievement. The respective mean scores of men and women are as follows: reading 25.68, 27.40, writing 17.09, 20.07, numeracy 16.74, 19.17 and total achievement 59.51 and 66.64.
11. Age has significantly influenced the achievement of neo-literates to reading, writing, numeracy and total achievement. Better performance scores were obtained 15-25 years and 26-35 years age groups than 35 years and above age group in all the cases. The respective mean scores of the age group (15-25 years, 25-35 years and 35 years and above) are follows: reading, 28.95, 26.21, 24.46, writing 21.90, 17.85, 15.99, numeracy 20.38, 17.65, 15.83 and total achievement 71.23, 61.71 and 56.28.
12. Caste has significantly influenced the achievement of neo-literates in literacy skills. Forward castes have secured a better mean achievement score duly followed by backward castes, scheduled castes and scheduled tribes in all the sub-tests and total

achievement. The respective scores of the three groups are reading: 29.71, 26.76 and 23.15; writing: 25.45, 17.65 and 15.57; numeracy: 20.24, 17.94 and 15.72; Total achievement: 75.40, 62.35 and 54.44.

13. Marital status has significantly influenced the achievement of neo-literates in case of reading, writing, numeracy and total achievement. The trend of mean scores indicated better achievement scores of married group in relation to their counterparts. The respective mean score of married and unmarried groups on the tests are as follows: Reading 28.00, 25.08, writing 20.25, 16.91, numeracy 19.52, 16.41 and total achievement 67.27 and 58.94.

14. Occupation has not significantly influenced the achievement of neo-literates with regard to reading, writing, numeracy and total achievement. Better mean performance scores were secured by non-agriculture group in all the cases when compared with the agricultural group. The respective mean scores of the agriculture and non-agriculture group are as follows: Reading 27.08, 28.05, writing 18.46, 18.70, numeracy 17.82, 18.09 and total achievement 63.37 and 64.84.

15. Income has significantly influenced the achievement of neo-literates in reading, writing, numeracy and total achievement. The trend of the mean scores revealed better achievement scores of higher income group (Rs.10,000/- and above per year) in relation to low income group(below Rs.10,000/- per year). The respective mean scores of the high and low income groups on the tests are as follows: Reading, 27.75, 25.33, writing 19.91, 17.25, numeracy 18.91, 17.02 and total achievement 66.57 and 59.60.

16. The influence of Factor A on the achievement of neo-literates was found to be significant with respect to

reading, writing, numeracy and total achievement. The mean scores obtained by high, medium and low scoring groups of Factor A on: (*a*) reading test are 27.34, 26.62, 25.66; (*b*) writing test are 19.34, 18.81, 17.59; (*c*) numeracy test are 19.94, 17.62, 16.32; and (*d*) total achievement are 66.22, 61.83 and 60.79. Hence, it is clear that Factor A significantly influenced their achievement. A person who scores high on Factor A tends to be warm hearted and out-going type i.e., the person tends to be good natured, easy going, ready to co-operate, attentive to people, trustful and adaptable.

17. The influence of Factor B on the achievement of neo-literates was found to be statistically significant. The trend of the means scores revealed that higher the level of Factor B scores better were the scores of the sample in reading, writing, numeracy and total achievement. The mean scores obtained by high, medium and low scoring group of Factor B on: (*a*) reading test are 28.25, 27.38, 23.99; (*b*) writing test are 20.10, 18.17, 17.49; (*c*) numeracy test are 20.40, 17.09, 16.40; and (*d*) total achievement are 68.75, 62.64 and 57.88. A person who scores high on Factor B tends to be quick grasper of ideas, fast learner and intelligent. He uses his insight and will be quick in adapting to circumstances. On the other hand, a person who scores low on Factor B tends to be slow to learn and grasp, dull and sluggish.

18. The influence of Factor C on the achievement of neo-literates in reading, writing, numeracy and total achievement was found to be statistically not significant. The mean scores obtained by high, medium and low scoring groups of Factor C on: (*a*) reading test are 29.87, 26.25, 23.52; (*b*) writing test are 19.09, 18.43, 18.22; (*c*) numeracy test are 18.38, 18.09, 17.41; and (*d*) total achievement are 66.37, 62.77,

60.12. A person who scores high on Factors C tends to be emotionally mature, stable, calm, pragmatic, realistic about life, placid and possesses ego strength. Further, he has the capacity to maintain high group morale. In contrast, a person who scores low on Factor C tends to be emotionally immature, easily perturbed, evasive of responsibilities, worrying and getting involved in unnecessary problem situations.

19. The influence of the Factor E on achievement of neo-literates in reading, writing, numeracy and total achievement was found to be statistically not significant. The mean scores obtained by high, medium and low scoring groups on the Factor E on: (*a*) reading test are 25.11, 26.26, 28.25; (*b*) writing test are 18.10, 18.27, 19.38; (*c*) numeracy test are 17.36, 18.08, 18.45; and (*d*) total achievement are 60.57, 62.61 and 66.08. As per descriptions a person who scores high on the factor tends to be ascendant, self-assured, assertive, independent minded and bold in his approach to situations. Further, he may at times be hard, stern, hostile, tough minded authoritarian in his approach. In contrast, a person who scores low on the factor tends to be a dependent, a follower and goes along with the groups. He tends to lean on others in making decisions and will be often soft hearted. He appears to be expressive and easily upset.

20. The influence of the Factor F on achievement of neo-literates in reading, writing, numeracy and total achievement was found to be statistically significant. The mean scores obtained by high, medium and low scoring groups on the Factor F on: (*a*) reading test are 27.19, 26.71, 25.72; (*b*) writing test are 19.10, 18.69, 17.85; (*c*) numeracy test are 23.25, 17.49, 13.25; and (*d*) total achievement are 68.54, 62.89 and 56.82. As per descriptions an individual who scores low on Factor F tends to be taciturn, reticent, and

introspective. Sometimes he will be incommunicative, pessimistic, anxious, depressed and slow. On the other hand, an individual who scores high on the factor tends to be cheerful, talkative, frank, expressive, quick, alert and unperturbable.

21. The influence of the Factor G on achievement of neo-literates in reading, writing, numeracy and total achievement was found to be statistically not significant. The mean scores obtained by high, medium and low scoring groups on the Factor G on: (*a*) reading test are 29.30, 25.65, 24.69; (*b*) writing test are 19.85, 18.54, 17.25; (*c*) numeracy test are 19.40, 17.78, 16.70); and (*d*) total achievement are 68.55, 61.97 and 58.64. As per the description of the traits of Factor G, a person who scores high on the factor tends to be strong in character, persevering, responsible, determined, consistent, planful, energetic, cautious and well organised. Usually he will be cautious with high regard for moral standards and prefers efficient people to other companions. On the other hand, a person who scores low on the factor tends to be fickle, undependable, irresolute and unsteady. He is sometimes demanding, impatient, obstructive and lacks internal standards.

22. The influence of the Factor H on achievement of neo-literates in reading, writing, numeracy and total achievement was found to be statistically significant. The mean scores obtained by high, medium and low scoring groups on the Factor H on: (*a*) reading test are 29.94, 25.87, 23.83; (*b*) writing test are 21.63, 19.20, 14.63; (*c*) numeracy test are 21.79, 17.59, 14.50; and (*d*) total achievement are 73.76, 62.66 and 53.26. A person who scores high on the Factor H tends to be sociable, adventurous, likes meeting people, active, responsive, friendly, impulsive, carefree and possesses capacity to face wear and tear in dealing

with people and grueling emotional situations without fatigue. In contrast, a person who scores low on the factor tends to be shy, withdrawing, cautious and cool. Further, he tends to be slow and impeded in speed and in expressing himself. He prefers one or two close friends to large groups and will not be able to keep in contact with all that happens around him.

23. The influence of the Factor I on achievement of neo-literates in reading, writing, numeracy and total achievement was found to be statistically not significant. The mean scores obtained by high, medium and low scoring groups on the Factor I on: (*a*) reading test are 25.05, 26.48, 28.09; (*b*) writing test are 18.13, 18.25, 19.37; (*c*) numeracy test are 17.44, 18.15, 18.30; and (*d*) total achievement are 60.62, 62.89, and 65.76. As per the description a person who scores high on Factor I tends to be tender minded, imaginative, introspective, artistic, fastidious and excitable. Sometimes he will be demanding, impatient, dependent and impractical. He tends to slow up group performances and to upset group morale by negative remarks. In contrast, a person who scores low on the factor tends to be practical, realistic, masculine, independent, responsible and cultured. Sometimes he will be hard, cynical and smug. He tends to keep a group operating on a practical and realistic basis.

24. The influence of the Factor L on achievement of neo-literates in reading, writing, numeracy and total achievement was found to be statistically not significant. The mean scores obtained by high, medium and low scoring groups on the Factor L on: (*a*) reading test are 25.74, 26.02, 27.86; (*b*) writing test are 18.30, 18.55, 18.89; (*c*) numeracy test are 17.45, 17.78, 18.65; and (*d*) total achievement are 61.49, 62.35, and 65.40. As per the description of factor traits, an

individual who scores low tends to be free of jealous tendencies, adaptable, cheerful, concerned about other people and a good team worker. On the other hand, an individual who scores high on the factor tends to be mistrusting and doubtful. Often he will be involved in his own ego, unconcerned about other people and a poor team worker.

25. The influence of the Factor M on achievement of neo-literates in reading, writing, numeracy and total achievement was found to be statistically significant. The mean scores obtained by high, medium and low scoring groups on the Factor M on: (*a*) reading test are 25.92, 26.15, 27.55; (*b*) writing test are 17.35, 18.58, 19.82; (*c*) numeracy test are 17.34, 18.15, 18.40; and (*d*) total achievement are 60.61, 62.88, and 65.77. As per the manual description a person who scores high on the factor tends to be conventional, unconcerned, bohemian, ego-centric, sensitive and imaginative. He sometimes makes emotional scenes, is some what irresponsible, impractical and undependable. He is often rejected in group situations. In contrast, a person who scores low on the factor tends to be anxious to do the right thing, practical and conformist. An examination of the traits indicate that for better academic achievement characteristics like being anxious to do right things, practical and conformist nature may help the learners. On the other hand, unconventional, unconcerned and ego-centric characteristics expressed by neo-literates may hamper their academic achievement.

26. The influence of the Factor N on achievement of neo-literates in reading, writing, numeracy and total achievement was found to be statistically significant. The mean scores obtained by high, medium and low scoring groups on the Factor N on: (*a*) reading test are 26.30, 26.06, 25.27; (*b*) writing test are 19.42, 18.47,

17.85; (*c*) numeracy test are 18.45, 18.16, 17.29; and (*d*) total achievement are 66.17, 62.69 and 60.14. As per the description, an individual who scores low on Factor N tends to be unsophisticated, sentimental and simple. He is easily pleased and sometimes crude and awkward. On the other hand, an individual who scores high on the factor tends to be polished, experienced, worldly and shrewd. He tends to be hard hearted and analytical. He has an intellectual, unsentimental approach to situations.

27. The influence of the Factor O on achievement of neo-literates in reading, writing, numeracy and total achievement was found to be statistically significant. The mean scores obtained by high, medium and low scoring groups on the Factor O on: (*a*) reading test are 24.60, 25.92, 29.10; (*b*) writing test are 18.20, 18.25, 19.30; (*c*) numeracy test are 17.22, 18.28, 18.40; and (*d*) total achievement are 60.02, 62.45 and 66.68. As per the manual description a person who scores low on Factor O tends to be placid, calm with unshakable nerve. He has a mature, complete confidence in himself and in his capacity to deal with things. He will be realistic and secure. On the other hand, a person who scores high on the factor tends to be depressed, moody, a worrier, suspicious, broody and avoids people. He has a child like tendency to anxiety in difficulties. He does not feel accepted in groups or feel to participate. If a neo-literate possesses mature and complete confidence in himself and in his capacity to deal with things naturally his academic achievement will be better than the neo-literate who shows depressed, worried, suspicious, moody and grueling traits.

28. The influence of the Factor Q_1 on achievement of neo-literates in reading, writing, numeracy and total achievement was found to be statistically significant.

The mean scores obtained by high, medium and low scoring groups on the Factor Q_1 on: (*a*) reading test are 27.85, 26.47, 25.31; (*b*) writing test are 19.22, 18.55, 17.97; (*c*) numeracy test are 18.33, 17.79, 17.77; and (*d*) total achievement are 65.40, 62.89 and 60.99. As per the description, a person who scores low on Factor Q_1 tends to be overly cautious and moderate. He will oppose any change, inclined to go along with tradition and tends not to be interested in analytical intellectual thought. On the other hand, a person who scores high on Factor Q_1 tends to be interested in intellectual matters and fundamental issues. He frequently takes issues with ideas, either old or new. He tends to be more well informed, less inclined to moralize, and more inclined to experiment in life generally, and more tolerant of inconvenience.

29. The influence of the Factor Q_2 on achievement of neo-literates in reading, writing, numeracy and total achievement was found to be statistically not significant. The mean scores obtained by high, medium and low scoring groups on the Factor Q_2 on: (*a*) reading test are 25.40, 26.86, 27.38 (*b*) writing test are 18.11, 18.15, 19.38; (*c*) numeracy test are 17.16, 17.30, 19.44; and (*d*) total achievement are 60.67, 62.31 and 60.20. As per the description, a person who scores low on the factor prefers to work and make decisions with other people, likes and depends on social approval and admiration. He tends to go along with the group and may be lacking in resolution. In contrast a person who scores high on the factor tends to be independent, resolute, accustomed to going in his own way, making decisions and taking action on his own. Craving for social approval and admiration and inclination to go along with a group may help a learner to achieve better than the learner who shows much independence and is in the habit of going in

his own way. These may perhaps be the reasons for marginal superiority for the low scorers on the factor over the high scorers in their achievement scores.

30. The influence of the Factor Q_3 on achievement of neo-literates in reading, writing, numeracy and total achievement was found to be statistically not significant. The mean scores obtained by high, medium and low scoring groups on the Factor Q_3 on: (*a*) reading test are 27.95, 25.88, 25.81; (*b*) writing test are 19.10, 18.26, 18.08; (*c*) numeracy test are 18.74, 18.63, 16.53; and (*d*) total achievement are 65.79, 62.77 and 60.42. As per the description of factor traits, a person who scores low on the factor tends to lack will control and character stability. He is not too considerate, careful or conscientious. In contrast, a person scoring high on the factor tends to have strong control of his emotions and general behaviour, is inclined to be considerate, careful and possesses self-respect. From the description it can be assumed that controlling of emotions and showing carefulness in behaviour may be helpful to the learners to achieve better whereas lack of will control on the part of learners may hamper their academic achievement.

31. The influence of the Factor Q_4 on achievement of neo-literates in reading, writing, numeracy and total achievement was found to be statistically not significant. The mean scores obtained by high, medium and low scoring groups on the Factor Q_4 on: (*a*) reading test are 25.46, 26.36, 27.80; (*b*) writing test are 17.62, 18.15, 19.18; (*c*) numeracy test are 17.75, 17.85, 18.30; and (*d*) total achievement are 60.93, 62.46 and 66.08. As per the description of the factor traits, an individual who scores low on the factor tends to be calm, relaxed, composed and satisfied. In contrast, an individual who scores high on the factor tends to be tense, excitable, restless and impatient. He is often

over fatigued. Further, he takes poor view of group unity, orderliness and leadership. If the learners possess majority of the traits attributed to the high scores on the factor, they may hamper their achievement.

32. The influence of the attitude on achievement of neo-literates in reading, writing, numeracy and total achievement was found to be statistically significant. The mean scores obtained by high, medium and low scoring groups on the attitude on: (*a*) reading test are 30.48, 27.51, 21.63; (*b*) writing test are 21.03, 19.43, 15.28; (*c*) numeracy test are 19.96, 17.27, 16.65; and (*d*) total achievement are 71.47, 64.21 and 53.56.

33. The orders of high correlations with reading achievement are as follows: Factor B (0.50), Attitude (0.45), Income (0.37), Caste (0.29), Factor Q_1 (0.25), Age (0.21), Factor A (0.21), Marital status (0.20), Factor E (0.18), Factor M (0.18), Factor Q_3 (0.18), Factor A (0.17), Factor H (0.16), Factor F (0.15), Factor Q_2 (0.15), Factor N (0.13), Gender (0.12), Factor C (0.12), Factor L (0.12), Factor G (0.11), Factor I (0.11), Factor Q_4 (0.08), Factor O (0.05).

34. The orders of high correlation with writing achievement are as follows. Attitude (0.44), Age (0.35), Factor A (0.31), Factor B (0.25), Caste (0.22), Factor I (0.22), Factor Q_1 (0.18), Income (0.16), Factor F (0.15), Factor E (0.13), Factor C (0.12), Factor M (0.12), Factor O (0.12), Marital status (0.11), Factor Q_2 (0.11), Gender (0.10), Occupation (0.08), Factor G (0.08), Factor N (0.08), Factor Q_3 (0.04), Factor L (0.02), Factor Q_4 (0.02).

35. The orders of high correlation with numeracy achievement are as follows. Factor B (0.41), Attitude (0.38), Factor H (0.26), Marital status (0.24), Income (0.18), Factor F (0.18), Factor A (0.17), Factor Q_3 (0.17),

Factor N (0.15), Factor I (0.14), Factor Q_2 (0.14), Caste (0.13), Factor E (0.13), Factor Q_4 (0.13), Occupation (0.12), Factor C (0.12), Factor O (0.12), Factor L (0.12), Factor M (0.11), Factor Q_1 (0.11), Age (0.08), Factor G (0.08) and Gender (0.05).

36. The orders of high correlation with total achievement are as follows. Factor B (0.41), Attitude (0.38), Factor H (0.26), Marital status (0.24),Income (0.18), Factor E (0.15), Factor A (0.15), Age (0.13), Factor F (0.13), Factor N (0.12), Factor G (0.12), Factor I (0.11), Factor Q_4 (0.14), Caste (0.11), Factor C (0.11), Factor Q_3 (0.10), Occupation (0.08), Factor L (0.08), Factor O (0.07), Gender (0.06), Factor Q_1 (0.05),Factor Q_2 (0.04), Factor Q_4 (0.04).

37. Out of 23 independent variable considered for analysis i.e., gender, age, caste, occupation, marital status, income, Factor A, Factor B, Factor C, Factor E, Factor F, Factor G, Factor H, Factor I, Factor L, Factor M, Factor N, Factor O, Factor Q_1, Factor Q_2, Factor Q_3, Factor Q_4, attitude only 6 variables were significantly related and explained 42.72 per cent of variance in the reading achievement. The contribution of each of the predictor variables was Factor B (11.10 per cent), attitude (10.61 per cent), income (1.78 per cent), caste (10.50 per cent), Factor Q_1 (4.08 per cent) and age (4.56 per cent).

38. Out of 23 independent variables considered for analysis, only 6 variables were significantly related and explained 38.26 per cent of variance in the writing achievement of neo-literates. The contribution of the variables is attitude 16.85, age 3.01, Factor A 8.53, Factor B 5.25, caste 1.97, Factor Q_1 2.65.

39. Out of 23 independent variables considered for analysis, only 5 variables were significantly related and explained 35 per cent of variance in the numeracy

achievement of neo-literates. The contribution of the variables is Factor B 10.00, attitude 9.00, Factor H 7.00, marital status 3.00, income 6.00.

40. Out of 23 independent variables considered for only 6 variables were significantly related and explained 47.35 per cent of variance in the total achievement of neo-literates. The contribution of the variables is attitude 26.92, Factor B 9.32, income 3.58, age 1.05, marital status 2.24, Factor G 4.24.

Implications of the Study

1. As the study reveals, the literacy attainment of neo-literates is 63.33 percent. Hence, it is necessary to concentrate on the neo-literates who could not attain the minimum levels in literacy. More emphasis has to be laid on writing and numeracy skills.
2. In the present study, it was found that the achievement of women learners was better in relation to men groups. Hence, efforts should be made to enhance the literacy levels of men learners by the district administration.
3. As far as the achievement of learners based on age is concerned, the learners in the 15-35 years age group have fared well in relation to other age group i.e., 35 years and above. Hence, stress should be laid on 35 years and above age group as well in promoting literacy skills.
4. It was found through the study that the performance of forward castes is better than the backward castes, scheduled castes and scheduled tribes. Hence efforts showed be made to extend the educational opportunities to the backward castes, scheduled castes and scheduled tribes.
5. With respect to marital status the married group of learners have achieved better scores in literacy skills.

Hence, emphasis should be laid on unmarried group in promoting literacy skills through effective organization of evening classes.

6. The study revealed that the performance of non-agricultural group (tailoring, brick making, business activities) was good in relation to agricultural group. Hence, efforts showed be made to cover the learners representing agricultural occupation.
7. It was observed through the study that the neo-literates having a monthly income of Rs.10,000 above have achieved better marks in the literacy test in relation to those having monthly income below Rs. 10,000. Hence, it is necessary to concentrate on lower income group in promoting literacy skills.
8. Personality factors like readiness to co-operate, attention, intelligence, sociability, emotional maturity, expression, cheerfulness, adaptability, interest in intellectual matters and fundamental issues strong in character craning for social approval etc. ,(represented by Factor A, B, F, G, H, Q_1) have contributed for better achievement. Personality factors like dull and sluggish nature, undependable aloofness, forgetful nature, stiffness, moodiness, rigidity, depressed nature, inconsistency, shyness, mistrusting, doubtful, ego-centric characteristics have contributed to low achievement. Hence it is suggested that attention should be paid basically to understand the learners, their needs and to mould to learning environment. Understanding the psychology of the learners should form as the basis and if once learner is self motivated he will continue to learn and what is needed is creation of conductive learning environment. It is necessary to stress about the learner aspects in the training programmes of the functionaries especially at the grassroot levels. The method of teaching should be learner oriented and

low cost methods of teaching should be used to arouse interest and creativity in the learners.

9. It was observed through the study that the attitude has significantly influenced the performance of neo-literates in literacy skills. Hence, steps should be taken to change the mind set of neo-literates on various aspects relating to literacy and continuing education programmes. It is necessary to launch motivational campaigns, provide and based learning materials, and organise income generating programmes.

Suggestions for Further Research

1. An exclusive research study can be carried out by considering other variables like participation in self help groups, mass media, exposure moral values, creativity, aptitude etc., on the performance of neo-literates.
2. A study may be carried out on performance of neo-literates in relation to learners perceptions about the qualities of volunteers/preraks.
3. A comparative study on performance of neo–literates may be considered keeping in view the districts where total literacy campaigns have proved to be highly successful and unsuccessful with a view to take up remedial measures.
4. A study on the social, economic, academic and psychological problems on the performance of neo-literates may be undertaken.
5. Indepth studies related to adult learning touching upon policy implications, materials, training and administration may be attempted.

Bibliography

Adult Basic Education Office, Pakistan (1973), *Interim Report of the Life-long Literacy Project Abstract in the Problems of Dropouts*, Tehran: International Institute for Adult Literacy Methods.

Ahmad (1958) *"An Evaluation of Reading Materials for Neo-literates and a Study of Their Reading Needs and Interests"*, New Delhi, Jamia Milia Islamia Research, Training and Production Centre.

Ahmad, Mushtaq (1965) What Literacy Does to People, *Indian Journal of Adult Education*, XXVI (10) October, pp.2-3 & 10-16.

Aikara, J. (1984). *Adult Education Programme in Maharashtra: An Appraisal*. Bombay, Unit for Research in the Sociology of Education, Tata Institute of Social Sciences.

Aikara, J. and Herniques (1982). *Functioning of the Adult Education Programme in Maharashtra*, Bombay, Tata Institute of Social Sciences.

Andhra University, Vizag (1994), *Evaluation of Literacy Campaign of Srikakulam District*, Department of Adult Education.

Anuradha, S. (1988). Developing Positive Attitudes Among Adult Education Functionaries, *Indian Journal of Adult Education*, Vol. 49, No. 2.

Arun Mishra and K.C. Kosthyal (1988). A Study of Attitude of Instructors Towards Adult Education, *Indian Journal of Adult Education*, Vol. 49, pp. 35.38.

Austin, M.J. (1982) "*Evaluating Your Agency's Programme*", Sage Publishers, London.

Berke, K. (1970), *Provisional Bibliography of Literacy Research,* Literacy Discussion, 11ALM, Vol. 1, No.3, Summer, pp.2-6

Best, J.W. (1959). Research in Education, USA. Prentice Hall, Inc., Englewood Cliffs, p.31.

Brist, (1983). *A Study of the National Adult Education Programme in the Tribal Region of Orissa State,* Ph.D. Education, M.S. University, Baroda.

Bhandari, J.S. and Mehta, R.C. (1974). Sources of Information, Motivation and Discouragement in Relation to the Adult Literacy Classes, *Indian Journal of Adult Education,* Vol. 35(11), pp. 98.110.

Bhingarkar, D.B. (1981) *Implication of the Concept of Life-long Education for Social Education,* Ph.D. Education, Bombay University.

Bhola, H.S (1967): 'Research in Adult Literacy', *Indian Journal of Adult Education;* XXV IV(9), pp.5-7.

Bikaner Adult Education Association (1973). *Evaluation Study, Adult Literacy Project,* Bikaner.

Bishit, A.R. (1983). Dropping out Phenomenon in Adult Education, *Indian Journal of Adult Education,* New Delhi, Vol. 44, No. 5, May.

Borg W.R. (1965) "*Educational Research – An Introduction*" New York; David McKay Company, Inc.

Brookfield, S.D. (1987) *Developing Critical Thinkers.* Jossey-Bass, San Francisco.

Brookfield, S. D. (1991) The Development of Critical Reflection in Adulthood. *New Education.* 13 (1): 39-48.

Collard, S. Law, M. (1989) The Limits of Perspective Transformation: A Critique of Mezirow's Theory. *Adult Ed. Q.* 39 (2): 99-107

Das, Manoranjan. (1990): *A Study of the Socio-economic Problems in the Implementation of the Adult Education programmes in Assam,* Ph.D., Education, Guwahati University. Denzil Saldanha (1993) " Evaluation on Latur District (Maharastra) Literacy Campaign". Unit for Research in Sociology of Education, TISS, Bombay

Denzil Saldhana (1992): *"The Total Literacy Campaign is Sindhudurg District"*; A Report of the evaluation. Tata Institute of Social Sciences, Bombay.

Department of Adult and Continuing Education and Extension (1985) Orientation/*Training Programme for Key Level Adult Education Functionaries*. Department of Adult and Continuing Education, Sri Venkateswara University, Tirupati.

Dey B.R. (1981) *"Adult Education Programme at the Patamata Block, Bihar"*, Directorate of Adult Education, Govt. of India, New Delhi.

Directorate of Adult Education (1973), *A Pilot Evaluation Study of Functional Literacy Project in Lucknow District* (Technical Report), New Delhi.

Dixit. (1975) "A Study of Educational Need Patterns of Adults in the urban, Rural and Tribal Communities of Rajastan", *Indian Journal of Adult Education*, Vol.36.

Durrell, D. (1958), "First Grade Reading Success Study a Summary", *Journal of Education*, 140(5), February.

Ekpenyong, L. E. (1990) Studying Adult Learning Through the History of Knowledge. *Int. J. Lifelong Educ.* 9

Ganguli, P. (1983). *Mode of National Adult Education Programme Follow-up Programme: A preliminary Study*, Patna. NAEP Evaluation Cell, A.N.S. Institute of Social Studies.

Ganguli, P. (1984) *Adult Education Through Universities* (A Case Study of Bihar University), Patna, NAEP Evaluation cell, A.N.S. Institute of Social Studies.

Gnanaseskhara Reddy (1999) *"Retention of Literacy Skills Among Neo-literates"*, M.A. Dissertation, Department of Adult Education, S.V. University, Tirupati.

Gokul, O. Parikh (1992): *"Adult Education Programme in Gujarat"* Sardar Patel Institute of Economic and Social Research, Ahmedabad.

Good, Barr, A.S. and Scates (1941). *Methodology of Educational Research*, New York, Appleton Century Crafts, Inc., pp. 10-18.

Goyal and Bhangoo (1988). Opinions of Adult Education Workers and Learners Regarding the Working of Adult Education Centres, *Indian Journal of Adult Education*, Vol. 49(2) April – June, pp. 39-54.

Grewel, J.S. (1992) *"Adult Education Programme in Andhra Pradesh State : An Evaluation Study"* NCERT, Regional College of Education, Bhopal.

Gupta, Premlal (1988). *Evaluation of Adult Literacy Centres in Relation to Their Programme Objectives in the State of Himachal Pradesh,* Ph.D. Education, Himachal Pradesh University.

Hebsur, F.K., Aikara, J. and Henriques, J. (1981). *National Adult Education programme in Maharashtra: An Evaluation,* Bombay: Tata Institute of Social Sciences.

Hand, S.E., Puder, W.H. (1968) *'A Preliminary Overview of Methods and Techniques in Adult Literacy and Adult Basic Education'*, The Florida Adult Educator, 18:1, April-September.

Haragopal and Ravindar (1980). Perceptions of the Key Functionaries about National Adult Education Programme. A Critical Appraisal, Indian Journal of Adult Education, Vol. 41(5), pp. 3-6.

Harihar, R. and Rao, T.V. (1982). *Adult Education in Rajasthan.* Third Appraisal (Jhunjhnu District), Ahmedabad, Public Systems Group, Indian Institute of Management, August, 1982.

Hebsur, R.K. Aikara, J. Herniques (1981). *National Adult Education Programme in Maharashra; An Evaluation,* TISS, Bombay.

Hemanta Kumar Khandai (2003) *"Psychology and Research in Adult Education"*. The Associated Publishers 293/2, Kacha Bazar, Post Box No. 56, Ambala Cantt. - 133 001 (India) Phone :0171 - 2618613.

Indra Deva and *et al.,* (1992); *"Narsinghpur Total Literacy Campaign, Report on Evaluation of Learning Outcomes"*. Conducted by External Evaluation Team. National Literacy Mission Authority, Ministry of Human Resource Development, Government of India, New Delhi.

Indra Deva and Rajasekhar (1993) *"Evaluation of Literacy Campaign, Bilaspur, Madhya Pradesh"*, cited in Evaluation of Literacy Campaigns, Summary Reports, Government of India, New Delhi.

Institute for Development Research and Alternatives (2001). *Evaluation of Akshara Sankrathi programme in Khammam District.* Associate of Sarvodaya Women Welfare Society. 518, Balaji Colony, Tirupati—517 502.

Jagannadha Sarma, K. *et.al.* (1998) Concurrent Evaluation of Continuing Education Programme, Report of Bench Mark Survey of West Godavari District, State Resource Centre for Adult Education, Literacy House, Andhra Mahila Sabha, Hyderabad.

Jagannadha Sarma, K. *et.al.* (1999) Concurrent Evaluation of Continuing Education Programme, Ranga Reddy District, Report of Bench Mark Survey, State Resource Centre for Adult Education, Literacy House, Andhra Mahila Sabha, Hyderabad.

Janaradhan Naidu (1980). *A Study of Farmers Attitudes Towards National Adult Education Programme in Srikalahasti Project*, M.A. Adult Education Dissertation, S.V. University, Tirupati.

Janardhan Rao, P. (2002) *The Problems Faced by Neo-literates and Volunteers in Continuing Education Programme of Chittoor district*, M.A. Dissertation, Dept. of Adult Education, S.V. University, Tirupati.

Janardhan Reddy, D. (1987). Persuasion of Adult Learners: A Study on Factors Motivating the Learners to Join Adult Education Centres as Perceived by the Instructors, *Indian journal of Adult Education, Vol. 40(3)*, pp. 39.43.

Janardhan Reddy, D. (1991). A Study of Certain Factors Related to Persisters and Dropouts of Adult Education, Ph.D., Department of Adult Education, S.V. University.

Janardhana Naidu. G (1982), *A Study of the Educational Problems of the Participants in Non-formal Education Centres in Karvetinagar Block*, M.Ed. Dissertation, Department of Education, Sri Venkateswara University, Tirupati.

Jayagopal, R. (1985) *Adult Learning (A Psychological Analysis in Indian Context)*, Dept. of Adult and Continuing Education, University of Madras.

Jersild, A.T., (1963): *The Psychology of Adolescence*, 2nd Ed. New York: Macmillan.

Kapoor, J.M. and Roy, p. (1971). Retention of Literacy Social Change, *Journal of the Council for Social Development*, 1, Aug, pp. 37-51.

Khajapeer, M. (1978). *A Study of the Academic Performance of the Farmers Functions Literacy Programme Participants in Relation to Socio-psychological Factors*, Ph.D Education, S.V. University.

Khatun, S.A. (1991). *A Study of the Problems of Adult Learners of the Rural Functional Literacy centres in the District of Cuttack*, M.Phil., Education, Utkel University.

Kitchener, K.S. King, P.M. (1990) The Reflective Judgment Model: Transforming Assumptions About Knowing. In: Mezirow J (ed.) *Fostering Critical Reflection in Adulthood*. Jossey-Bass, San Francisco.

Krishna Murthi Bh., *et al* (1992) *"Evaluation of the Total Literacy Campaign in Chittoor District: A Report"*, University of Hyderabad, Hyderabad.

Kumaraswamy, T. (2007) *External Evaluation Report of Akshara Bharathi Programme Phase – II, Medak District*, Andhra Pradesh, Department of Adult and Continuing Education, Sri Venkateswara University, Tirupati.

Kumaraswamy, T. (1992) *"A Study of Certain Factors Related to Achievement of Adult Learners"*, Ph.D. Thesis in Dept. of Adult and Continuing Education, S.V. University, Tirupati – 517 502, Andhra Pradesh, India.

Kulasekhar, K. (2005) *A Study of Certain Aspects of Continuing Education Programme in Chittoor District* (Andhra Pradesh), with Special Reference to Tribals, Ph.D. Thesis, Department of Adult and Continuing Education, S.V. University, Tirupati.

Kumarswamy, T. and Surendra, G. (2004). *A Study on the Performance of Tribal Women in Khammam District*. Tribal Development Studies, The Associated Publishers Ambala, Cantt., pp.360-369.

Kumarswamy, T. and Robert Dev Doss, V. (2002). *Motivational Aspects of Literacy Campaigns, UGC National Seminar on Literacy and Development Through Voluntarism*, Compendium of Papers, Department of Adult and Continuing Education, S.V. University, Tirupati.

Lakshiminarayana P.Ch (1983) *"A Study of Adult Education Among Tribals of Visakhapatnam District of Andhra Pradesh"* Ph.D. Thesis, Dept. of Adult Education, Andhra University, Visakhapatnam.

Lal, M and Mishra, R (1982). *Adult Education in Bihar, Patna*, A.N.S. Institute of Social Studies.

Lokanadha Reddy (1981), "*A Study of Certain Personality Characteristics of Active Participants and Drop-outs Enrolled in Adult Education Centres of Sri Kalahasti Project*", Chittoor District, (A.P), M.A. Dissertation, Department of Adult and Continuing Education, S.V.University, Tirupati.

London, Jack (1970); *Adult Education in Tanzamia: An Approach to its Development.* Dares Salaam Institute of Adult Education, University College.

Madhavi, K. (1988) *Problems of Adult Women in Attending the Adult Education Centres.* M.A. Dissertation, Department of Adult Education, Sri Venkateswara University, Tirupati.

Manjula, A.(1986) *An Enquiry into the Problems of Adults in Learning Process,* M.A. Adult Education, Dissertation, Department of Adult and Continuing Education, Sri Venkateswara University, Tirupati.

Mustaq Ahmed (1992); "*An Evaluation of Total Literacy Campaign of Midnapur District (West Bengal),* National Literacy Mission Authority, New Delhi..

Madana Mohan Reddy, C. (1980) "*Attitude of Adult Learners towards National Adult Education Programme*", M.A. Dissertation, Department of Adult Education, S.V.University, Tirupati.

Madras Institute of Development Studies (1982). *Adult Education Programme in Tamil Nadu: An appraisal of the Role of the State Government, Madras.*

Mariappan, Suseela and Ramakrishnan (1981). *An Evaluative Study of the National Adult Education Programme in the Union Territory of Pondicherry,* State Resource Centre for Non-formal Education, Madras.

Mastan, V. (2000). *Influence of Training, Attitude and Community Support on the Performance of Preraks Organizing* Continuing Education Centres, M.Phil. in Education. Alagappa University, Karaikudi.

Mathur, K.(1976) *Evaluation Study*: 1975-76, Bikanir, Bikaner Adult Educational Association, 53.

Mezirow J (1991) *Transformative Dimensions of Adult Learning.* Jossey-Bass, San Francisco

Mohan, A. (1983) *Opinion of Instructors about Get-up and Contents of Health and Sanitation Reader used in National Adult Education Programme*, M.A. Dissertation, Department of Adult Education, S.V. University, Tirupati.

Mohanty, N. (1988). *Evaluation of the Functional Literacy Programme in Puri District, Orissa,* M.Phil., Education, University of Poona.

Munuswamy (1980). *The Attitude of the Adult Education Instructors towards the National Adult Education Programme in Srikalahasti Block*, M.A. in Adult Education, Dissertation, S.V. University, Tirupati.

Mushtaq Ahmad (1991) *"A Few Observations on the Post Literacy Campaign of Burdwan District"* (Mimeo) Zilla Saksharatha Samithi, Burdwan.

Muthayya, B.C and Hemalatha, C. (1980). *Implementation of National Adult Education Programme*, National Institute of Rural Development, Hyderabad.

Muthayya, B.C. (1971). *Farmers and Their Aspirations*, Hyderbad, National Institute for Rural Development.

Naidu, K. Jaya Chandrama. (1986). *A Comparative Study of the Academic Achievement of the Students of Formal and Non-formal Education*, Ph.D. Education, S.V. University, Tirupati.

Naik, J.P. (1979). "A Quick Appraisal of National Adult Education Programme in Gujarat", *Indian Journal of Adult Education* Vol.40, No.2, February. pp.1-4.

Nanda, T.J.K. Beri (1974) Advantages of Literacy as Perceived by Adults Attending Adult Literacy Centres in Patiala Circle, *Indian Journal of Adult Education*, Vol. 35(1), p.17.

Naresh Sharma, K.L. Dangia and Vishakha Bansa (2001) "Attitude of Adult Beneficiaries toward Total Literacy Campaign, Dungarpur District of Rajasthan", *Indian Journal of Adult Education* Vol. 62, No.2, April-June, 2001,pp.32-36.

Nath, T.S.J.C. (1981) "Attitude of NSS Adult Education Organisers towards National Adult Education Programme", M.A. *Dissertation, Department of Adult Education*, S.V. University, Tirupati.

Obulesu, M.C. (2001). *An Enquiry into the Problems of Dropouts in Total Literacy Campaign of Kurnool District*, Ph.D. Thesis, Department of Adult and Continuing Education, S.V. University, Tirupati.

Om Mehata, Billore, Dave and Sharma. (1994) *Evaluation of Literacy Campaign, Durg as Referred in Evaluation of Literacy Campaigns,* Summary Reports, Vol. 1 (12-13), New Delhi, Directorate of Adult Education, Govt. of India.

Pabitra and Others (1993). *Total Literacy Campaign in South 24 Paraganas of West Bengal*, Unpublished Evaluation Report, Directorate of Adult Education, New Delhi.

Patel, B., Raman and D.N. Pandya (1974). Farmers Motives to Join Training Classes, *Indian Journal of Adult Education*, Vol. 35(12), pp.105-106.

Pestonjee, D.M. Laharia, S.N. and Dixit, D, (1981), *National Adult Education Programme in Rajasthan*, Second Appraisal, Indian Institute of Management. Ahmedabad.

Pillai, K.S. (1976). *"The Impact of Literacy Programmes on Women Learners in Kerala*, Prasar, 3(4) January, pp. 12.15.

Pabitra *et. al* (1993): *"Hooghly Zilla Sarbit Zakcharath (1993)" Towards Total Literacy (An Evaluation of Hooghly Compaign)* Hooghly, West Bengal. Draft Report.

Prakash, Brahma, (1978). *The Impact of Functional Literacy in the Rural Areas of Haryana and Union Territory of Delhi.* Ph.D. Education, Kurukshetra University.

Rajan, R. (1992). *A Critical Study of the Mass Programme of Functional Literacy in Tamil Nadu*, Ph.D., Education University of Poona.

Rajyalakshmi, K. (1986). Non-formal Education, Discovery Publishing House, New Delhi.

Ram Devi, S. *et.al.* (1971) *On Getting People to Participate: Seven Case Studies*, New Delhi, Central Institute of Research in Public Co-operation, 161, P+Appex.

Ramabrahmam *et.al.* (1997). *Evaluation of Total Literacy Campaign in East Govdavari District – A Report.* The University of Hyderabad, P.O. Central University, Hyderabad.

Ramachandra, V. (1994). *Reading Proficiency of Learners in Total Literacy Campaign of Chinnagottigallu Mandal,* M.Phil, Dissertation, Department of Adult Education, S.V. University, Tirupati.

Ramakrishnan, K. *et.al.* (1993). *Total Literacy Campaign in the Union Territory of Pondicherry, An Evaluation,* Bharthair University, Coimbatore.

Ramana Reddy, G. and Adinarayana Reddy, P.(1995) A Study of the Participation of Village Co-ordinators in Implementation of Total Literacy Campaign in Chittoor District, *Indian Journal of Adult Education,* New Delhi, Vol. 56, No. 1, pp. 40-45.

Rao, A.D.S and Padma, N. (1958). *A Study of the Interests of illiterate Adults in Srikrishna Rajendra Mills* (Mysore: Mysore State Adult Education Council).

Rao, B.S. Vasudeva (1983). *National Adult Education Programme in Visakhapatnam District,* A Study of Differential Impact, Ph.D., Adult Education, Andhra University, Waltair.

Rao, B.S. (1979). "Literacy by Tribals", *Indian Journal of Adult Education,* 40(4).

Rajani R.Shirur (1997) "*A Synergy of Theory, Practice and Strategies in Adult Learning*", Sterling Publishers Private Limited, L-10, Green Park Extension, New Delhi - 110016, pp. 27, 28, 30, 31.

Rajendrudu, S. (2005) *A Study on the Performance of Adult Learners, M.A. Adult Education,* Dissertation, Department of Adult and Continuing Education, Sri Venkateswara University, Tirupati - 517 502,

Ramakrishna, K. *et al.,* (1993) "*Total Literacy Campaign in the Union Territory of Pondicherry, An Evaluation;* Bharathiar University, Coimbatore.

Rao, T.V., Bhatta, T.P. Rao, Rama (1980). *Adult Education for Social Change,* Manohar Publications, Delhi.

Reddeppa (2001). *A Study on Jana Chaitanya Kendras (JCKs) in Chittoor District with Special Reference to Monitor Effectiveness,* Ph.D. in Adult Education, S.V. University, Tirupati.

Reddy, (1980). An Enquiry into Some Factors Related to Concept Attainment-based on Clue Variation Among Literate and Illiterate Adults, M.A. Dissertation, Adult Education, S.V. University.

Reddy, M.V. Sudhakara (1980). A Study of Certain Factors Related to the Development of Conceptual Generalization (Concept Learning) Among Adults, Ph.D. Psychology, S.V. University.

Reddy, P.A. (1990). A Study of Certain Socio-psychological Factors relating to Adult Education Instructor Effectiveness, Doctoral Dissertation, Department of Adult Education, S.V. University.

Rogers Alan, (1986) Teaching Adults, Open University Press. Milton Keynes, Philadelphia.

Roy Pradipto and Kapoor, J.M. (1975) *The Retention of Literacy, New Delhi*, Council for Social Development, Macmillan

Salamathuallah and Bareth, S.D. (1984). *Adult Education Research in India: A Study*, Indian Adult Education Association, New Delhi.

Sambhalpur University (P.G. *Department of Anthropology*), Orissa (1992). Evaluation of Literacy Campaign, Ganjam District.

Sampoornam, R. (2004), *Academic Performance of Non-formal Education Learners in relation to Socio-economic Factors*, Ph.D, Thesis Department of Adult and Continuing Education, Sri Venkateswara University, Tirupati – 517 502.

Sardar Patel Institute of Economic and Social Research , Ahmedabad (1994), National Literacy Campaign, *Cited in Evaluation of Literacy Campaigns*, Summary Report, Government of India, New Delhi.

Sardar Patel Institute of Economic and Social Research (1993) *Evaluation of Literacy campaign, Kuch District*, Khedia District, Gujarat, Ahmedabad.

Savicevic, D.M. (1991) Modern Conceptions of Andragogy: A European Framework. *Studs. in the Ed. of Adults*, 23(2):179-201.

Seth, M. (1981) Motivation in Adult Learners Participating in the Functional Literacy Programme in Delhi, Ph.D. Home Science, Delhi University.

Shankar, R. (1972). *An Experiment in Function Literacy Teaching through Naya Savera Method*, Literacy House, Lucknow.

Sharma, K.L. (1972). Attitudes towards Adult Education, *Indian Journal of Adult Education, Vol. XXXIII*, No. 12, December.

Simmons, J. (1972). *Towards an Evaluation of Adult Education and Literacy for Development*, Tunishian Experiment, Part-II.

Singh, T.R. (1975). *A Report on the Naya Savera Primer*, Literacy House, Lucknow.

Soujanya (1994). *Motivational Factors Influencing the Enrollment of Illiterates in the Literacy Centres under Literacy Campaign*, M.Phil., Departments of Adult Education, S.V. University, Tirupati.

Stanton, A. (1970). Provisional Bilbliography of Literacy Research, Literacy Discussion, 1(3) Summer, p.97.

Subramanyam, R. and Mani, R.S. (1964). "A Probe into Adults Attitude to Literacy: A Report of an Investigation", *Indian Journal of Adult Education*, Vol. XXV, No.5, May, pp. 11-15.

Sudha Rani, K., Surendra G. and Sampoorna, R (2003). Constraints in the Sustainability of Continuing Education Centres in India, *Indian Journal of Adult Education*, Vol. 64. No.2, April-June, pp. 66-68.

Sudhakara Reddy, M.V. (1997). *Total Literacy Campaign, Chitradurga District, Karnataka State*, External Evaluation Report, Department of Adults Continuing Education, S.V. University, Tirupati.

Sudhakara Reddy, M.V., Janardhana Reddy, D. and Kumaraswamy, T. (2004). *External Evaluation Report of Akshara Sankranthi (Phase-1), Prakasam District*, Department of Adult and continuing Education, S.V. University, Tirupati.

Surya Mani, P. and Reddy, S.V. (1985). Attitude and Job Satisfaction of Organizers Working Under Adult Education Programmes: A Study, *Indian Journal of Adult Education*, Vol. 36.

Swamy, T.K. (1980). *A Study of Certain Factors related to Concept Learning among Literate and Illiterate Adults Involving Familiar and Unfamiliar Material*, M.A., Dissertation, Dept. of Adult Education, S.V. University.

Sidda Gowda, Y.S.(1996) *Akshara Vani External Evaluation Report of Total Literacy Campaign*, Chitradurga, Karnataka, Department of Social Work, Mysore University, Manasagamgothri, Mysore – 570 006.

Smith R M (ed.) (1990) *Learning to Learn Across the Lifespan*. Jossey-Bass, San Francisco.

State Resource Centre for Adult Education (1995), *An Evaluation Study of Total Literacy Campaign East Godavari District*. Literacy House, Andhra Mahila Sabha, Hyderabad – 500 007.

Susheela Mariaappan (1982) "Learners Attitude in Adult Education Centres of Tamil Nadu and Pondichery:, *Indian Journal of Adult Education*, Vol. 43, No.1, January, 1982, pp.19-20.

Talukdar.BK (1975) "*Adult Education in Assam during Post-independence Period*", Ph.D. Thesis, Dept, of Education, Gauhati University.

Tata Institute of Social Sciences, Bombay (1993). *External Evaluation of Literacy Campaign*, Latur, Maharashtra.

Thompson Ekundayo, J.D.(2001) "*Transforming the Adult Education Agenda through the Kenya Post-literacy Project*, Adult Education and Development, DVV, Institute of International Co-operation of the German Adult Education Association, Vol. 56, 2001.

Tribhuvan University (1982): "*Determinants of Educational Participation in Rural Nepal*", Research Centre for Educational Innovation and Development, Kathmandu, Nepal.

Tripathi V. (1981) *Post-literacy Activities Conceived in the Perspective of Life-long Education in India – A Case Study*, Directorate of Adult Education, New Delhi, Literacy House, Lucknow.

Umayaparvathi, S. (1982). *A Study of Achievement Motivation, Intelligence and Literacy Attainment in Some of the Urban and Rural Women's Literacy Centres in Tamil Nadu*, and Pondicherry States, Ph.D in Education, Department of Adult and Continuing Education, Madras.

University of Hyderabad (1992). *Evaluation of Literacy Campaign*, Nizamabad District.

University of Hyderabad (1992). *Evaluation of Literacy Campaign*, Chittoor District.

Varalakshmi, E. (1980). *An Enquiry into Certain Factors related to Concept Attainment among Adults-based on Rule Variation*, M.A. Adult Education Dissertation, S.V. University.

Vasudeva Rao, B. S. (1999) "Evaluation of Total Literacy Campaign in Nellore District of Andhra Pradesh" *Indian Journal of Adult Education*, New Delhi.

Vasudeva Rao, B.S. (1984) "*Adult and Continuing Education: Some Perspectives*", Rural Development Publications, Andhra Pradesh.

Vasudeva Rao, B.S, Viswanadha Gupta, P. and Srinivasa Rao (2005) *Akshara Bharathi Programme: Volunteers'Perceptions, Journal of Adult Education and Extention,* Dept. of Adult and Continuing Education, Sri Venkateswara University, Tirupati-517 502, Vol-1, No.2, July-Dec. 2005.

Vasudeva Rao, B.S. (1988) *"National Adult Education Programmes in Visakhapatnam District"*, Himalaya Publishing House, Delhi.

Vasudeva Reddy, (1983) *Opinion of the Instructors about the Get-up and Contents of the Primer-increase Your Income (Reader Used in NAEP), Tirupati,* M.A. Dissertation, Dept. of Adult Education, S.V. University, Tirupati.

Venkataiah, N. (1976) *Impact of Farmers Functional Literacy Programme on the Participants in Andhra Pradesh,* Ph.D. Education, S.V. University.

Venkatesulu, P. (1980). *A Study of Certain Factors Related to Concept Learning Among Adults-based on Variations in rule Learning,* M.A. Dissertation, Adult Education, S.V. University.

Verma, Mishra and Lal (1981). Adult Education for Development, *A Study of the National Adult Education Programme in Bihar,* Patna, A.N. Sinha Institute of Social Sciences.

Vijayalakshmi (1985). *Opinion of Adult Education Instructors about their Profession and Adult Education in General,* M.A. Dissertation, S.V. University, Tirupati.

Visaria, L. and Mathew, T. (1983). Adult Education Programme in Gujarat, Fourth Evaluation, Ahmedabad, Sardar Patel Institute of Economic and Social Research.

Vooglaid Y, Marja, T. (1992) Andragogical Problems of Building a Democratic Society. *Int. J. of Lifelong* Ed 11(4):321-328.

Wilson and Reddy (1979), Attitude of Teacher Volunteers towards Farmers Functional Literacy Programmes, *Indian Journal of Adult Education,* 40(6), pp.29-33.

Yogananda Sastry, and Rajanikanth. G. (1992) *Evaluation of Literacy Crusade in Chittoor District* of Andhra Pradesh, National Institute for Rural Development, Hyderabad.

Index

A

Achievement in
- numeracy, 141
- reading, 140
- writing, 140-141

Adult Education for Women, 8
Adult Education through Universities and Colleges, 10
Adult Education Through Voluntary Agencies, 11
Adult learners, 76
Akshara Bharathi programme, 66
Akshara Tapasman, 23
Analysis of data, 95, 190
Andhra Pradesh, 23, 30, 58
Arjuna, 23
Attitude towards adult education, 78

B

Bharatha Gyana Vignana Samithi (BGVs), 25
Bikaner Adult Education Association (1973), 30
Boundaries and topography, 20
Burdwan Zilla Saksharata Samiti (1991), 32

C

China, 3
Chittor District, 19, 22
- climate, 21

Collection of data, 94-95, 190
Constitution of Education Commission (1964-66), 7
Content validity, 93
Continuing education, 78

D

Definition of certain terms, 75

E

Education Commission, 7
Equivalency programmes, 77

F

Farmers Functional Literacy Programme in Andhra Pradesh, 6, 30

Findings of the study, 190
Functional literacy, 76
Functions of continuing education centres, 17

G

Gender, age and occupation, 59
Government of Andhra Pradesh, 70, 184
Government of India, 8, 27
Gram Shikshan Mohim, 6
Guilford, 93

H

Hypotheses, 73, 187

I

Illiteracy, 182
Implications of the study, 204
Income generating programmes, 77
Individual interest promotion programmes, 77
Institute for Development Research and Alternatives, 36
Integrated Child Development Services, 8
Intrinsic validity, 93-94
Introduction, 1-27, 182
    education and national development, 1-3
    family and community living, 5
    health and hygiene, 5
    literacy and cultural activities, 5
    recreational activities, 5
    social education programme, 3-6
    vocations, 5
Irrigation, 22
Item validity, 93

J

Jana Chaitanya Kendras, 65
Jana Shikshan Sansthan, 18
Jana Shikshana Nilayams (JSNs), 13

K

Kenya Post-literacy Project, 64

L

Limitations, 75
Literacy activities in Chittor district, 22

M

Madras Institute of Development Studies (1982), 60
Mahabharata, 23
Maharashtra, 6
Mandal Literacy Organizers, 81
Mass Programme for functional Literacy, 12
Measure of achievement, 80-83
Measure of attitude, 88-90
Measure of personality, 87-88
Methodology, 80-95
Minerals, 22
Monitor, 76

N

Nation Adult Education Programme (NAEP), 9, 11, 59
National Literacy Mission, 13, 69, 191
National Literacy Mission Authority, 24
Need for the study, 184
Neo-literature, 75
Non-formal education, 8
Numeracy test, 85-86

O

Objectives of the study, 16, 73, 187
Osmania University, 23
Overview of adult education programmes after independence, 3

P

Performance/achievement, 76
Polyvalent Adult Education Centres, 8
Post-literacy, 78
  and continuing education, 15
Procedure of standardization, 91
Profile of Chittor District, 19

Q

Quality of life improvement programmes, 77

R

Rainfall, 21
Rating procedure for the statements, 90-91
Reading test, 83-84
Reliability of the measure, 92
Results and discussion, 96-181
  age vs. achievement, 109-110
  correlation matrices, 140
  correlation with achievement in
    numeracy, 141
    reading, 140
    writing, 140-141
  correlation with total achievement, 141-153
  distribution of
    numeracy achievement scores, 104-106
    performance scores, 100-102
    sample as per variables, 97-99
    total achievement scores, 106-108
    writing achievement scores, 102-104
  factor A vs. achievement, 117-118
  factor B vs. achievement, 118-119
  factor C vs. achievement, 119-121
  factor E vs. achievement, 121-122
  factor F vs. achievement, 122-123
  factor G vs. achievement, 123-128
  factor L vs. achievement, 128-129
  factor M vs. achievement, 129-130
  factor N vs. achievement, 130-133
  factor Q1 vs. achievement, 133-134
  factor Q2 vs. achievement, 134-135
  factor Q3 vs. achievement, 135-137
  factor Q4 vs. achievement, 137-138
  factors predicting achievement of neo-literates in
    numeracy, 169-174
    reading, 154-161
    writing, 161-168

factors predicting total achievement of neo-literates, 174-181

gender vs. achievement, 108-109

income vs. achievement, 115-116

influence of

attitude on achievement, 138-140

caste on achievement, 111-112

economic variables on achievement, 114

personal variables on achievement, 108

personality factors on achievement, 116-117

social variables on achievement, 111

literacy achievement among neo-literates as per NLM norms, 99-100

marital status vs. achievement, 112-113

multiple regression analysis, 154

occupations vs. achievement, 114-115

Review of related literature, 28-67

Ahmed, Mustaq, 32

Deva, Indra, 38

Dixit, 31

Grewal, 31

Herniques, 42

Nanda and Beri, 38

Pillai, 30

Rajendrudu, 35

Ramachandra, 33

Rao, Vasudeva, 42

Rao, Vasudeva, 34

Reddy, Sudhakar, 39

Shankar, 37

Venkataiah, 42

Rivers, 21

Rural Functional Literacy Project, 11

S

Sardar Patel Institute of Economic and Social Research (1994), 35

Scheduled Castes, 71, 185

Scheduled Tribes, 71, 185

Scope of the study, 72

Scoring of the statement, 91-92

Selection of the sample, 94, 189

Selection of the statements, 92

Shramik Vidyapeeths, 8

Social Education Programme, 1949, 183

Soils, 22

State Adult Education Programme, 11

Statement of the problem, 68-79, 184

need for the study, 68-72

Studies on attitude, 57

Dey, 60

Dixit, 58

Kukasekhar, 66

Kumaraswamy, 63

Lakshminarayana, 61

Mariappan, Susheela, 60

Mastan, 64

Mohan, 61

Munuswamy, 59

Ramabrahmam, 63

Reddeppa, 65

Reddy, Madana Mohana, 59
Seth, 61
Sharma, Naresh, 65
Thompson, 64
Venkataiah, 58
Studies on personal, social and economic factors, 29
Studies on psychological factors, 43
Bishit, 49
Khajapeer, 47
Khandai, Hemanta Kumar, 56
Lawton, 43
Lowe, 44
Manjula, 49
Reddy, 47
Shirur, Rajnani R, 55
Sinha, 44
Suggestions, 206

T

Tata Institute of Social Sciences, 34
Tools developed, 189
Total Literacy Campaign in Lathur, 34
Total Literacy Campaigns, 14

V

Validity and reliability, 87
Validity of the scale, 92-93
Variables studied, 74, 188
Voluntary Organizations, 9

W

Writing test, 84-85

Z

Zilla Sakharatha Samithi, Chittoor, 23, 75, 76